First Published 1925
Reprinted 1977

PRINTED IN THE UNITED STATES OF AMERICA

AMERICAN POETRY

1 9 2 5

A MISCELLANY

GRANGER BOOKS
MIAMI, FLORIDA

A FOREWORD

So many misconceptions have arisen concerning the origins, purposes, and scope of *American Poetry —A Miscellany,* that it may be well to restate, in some detail, its history and its aims.

During the year 1919 a group of American poets, meeting occasionally at various places, speculated upon the possibility of closer contact between themselves and their confrères. The very word "group" may be misleading, for these poets had no relation to each other beyond a respect for each other's work. At all events, it was agreed that a volume of new poems by a dozen representative native authors would have a certain value—particularly if that volume, instead of being an anthologist's selection, were to be composed by the poets themselves. It would give in each instance at least a true (and recent) picture of the individual contributor. And so, in 1920, after inviting four or five other poets, the first *Miscellany* appeared.

Its procedure was simple and its method was nothing more than the carrying out of the following four principles:

1. Coöperative participation and division of royalties, the royalties to be divided in proportion to the length of each poet's contribution.

2. New poems only. The *Miscellany* is not in-tended as an addition to the many anthologies gleaning the field of modern poetry. It will pre-sent only such poems as have not appeared in any previous volume by the author or, as far as possi-ble, in any other compilation. Not only does it purpose to print the poet's most recent work but, for the most part, it will contain verse that has not even been offered for publication.

3. No editor. Each contributor is to have twenty pages completely at his disposal; he is to be free to fill all or as many of them as he wishes.

4. New members to be added with each new issue. The newcomers are to be invited by consent (pref-erably unanimous) of the original contributors.

It should be added that these four principles were never incorporated in a program; outside of a letter or two, they were never reduced to a written formula. But they were implicit in the spirit as well as the production of the *Miscellany*. Despite the assertions of some of its critics, the *Miscellany* did not claim to be inclusive, for its object was neither the meri-torious one of attempting to be a compendium of present-day American verse nor the possibly more exciting one of furnishing an incubator for experi-mental talents. It presented obviously a limited list, a baker's dozen chosen from the roster of those who had "won their spurs." As the Foreword to the second *Miscellany* (1922) insisted: "It is as if a dozen unacademic painters, separated by temperament and distance, were to arrange to have an exhibition every two years of their latest work. They would not pretend that they were the only painters worthy of a public showing; they would maintain only that their work was representative of the artists and, generally speaking, most interesting to one another."

This collaborative spirit triumphed during the first two numbers. Some one had to collect the manuscripts, remind the members of the approaching date of publication, supervise the physical production of the book, assume charge of the business details, and this labor of correspondence and assembling was delegated to the writer of this explanation. But the principle of "No editor" was so jealously observed that even the brief Foreword required the collaboration of four poets.

With the growth of the *Miscellany* unforeseen difficulties interfered with the hitherto pleasant progress. The fourth principle proved particularly troublesome. It should have been obvious to all that no six people can ever agree on any one topic—and to demand unanimity from a dozen varied poets is more than even the most optimistic contributor could ever expect. It was. The separation "by temperament and distance" prevented the issuance of the *Miscellany* in 1924. Geography was chiefly responsible. With one contributor in England, another touring the Californian coast, a third in Switzerland, a fourth making a trip around the world, one letter lost, another tardily delivered, it became evident that, though most of the original aims could be preserved, a certain arbitrariness of action was necessary. Accordingly, the present writer's task of assembling the materials for the volume has been extended to include the addition of new members. This—in the present issue—he has done and, though former contributors were consulted, he assumes full responsibility for this feature.

The other principles, as well as the general objects, remain unchanged. At the risk of being redundant, the contributors insist that the *Miscellany* is not the organ of any school. It is not an attempt to throw into relief any particular group or stress any particular tendency. It is not formed—in sharp distinction to its English predecessor, *Georgian Poetry*—in accordance with any one temperament. Each poet, in his capacity of individual editor, has chosen and arranged his own representation, but he has had no authority over the choice or the grouping of his fellow-exhibitors' contributions.

Two facts may be added as matters of record: The new members of this year's *Miscellany* are William Rose Benet, T. S. Eliot, John Crowe Ransom, Wallace Stevens, and Elinor Wylie. In the first issue the contributors appeared in alphabetical order; in the second, seniority became the uncertain arbiter of precedence. It has been thought wise to revert to the original plan, and so the alphabet is again responsible for the arrangement.

A Foreword

Although all of these poems are presented in a volume for the first time,* some of them have appeared in recent magazines. Thanks for permission to reprint such selections are due to *The American Mercury, The Century, The Commonweal, The Dial, Harper's, Hearst's International, The Measure, The Nation, The New Republic, The North American Review, The Outlook* (London), *Poetry: A Magazine of Verse, The Saturday Review of Literature, Vanity Fair, The Yale Review.*

*   *   *   *   *

Since this foreword was written, the *Miscellany* —and American poetry—has lost one of its most valued contributors. After struggling for years against crippling odds, Amy Lowell died suddenly on May 12, 1925. Sharing the lot of all pioneers, she saw her verse become the butt of scorn and ridicule; unlike most innovators, however, she lived to see her work rise from the limbo of dubious experiment to the definite place which even her opponents have finally accorded her. Her death comes with a sense of personal loss to the group which these pages represent. It was at her home that the plans for the first *Miscellany* assumed actual form, and it was greatly due to her unflagging enthusiasm that the biennial was continued through a period of

---

* An exception to this statement is the group of sonnets by Edwin Arlington Robinson. These sonnets have just appeared in Mr. Robinson's latest volume, *Dionysus in Doubt,* published by The Macmillan Company, holders of the copyright.

A Foreword

difficult complexities. She was a champion of poetry and a friend of poets, and it is the loss of the friend as well as the passing of a provocative force that we mourn. Her group in the present *Miscellany* has a special significance, not only because it contains some of the last work Amy Lowell ever wrote, but because the poem "Mesdames Atropos and Clio Engage in a Game of Slap-Stick" refers to the exhaustive work on Keats which hastened her end.

Louis Untermeyer.

April, 1925.

CONTENTS

ix

Contents

x

Contents

Contents

Contents

xiii

Contents

CONRAD AIKEN

Conrad Aiken

THE ROAD

THREE then came forward out of darkness, one
An old man bearded, his old eyes red with weeping,
A peasant, with hard hands. "Come now," he said,
"And see the road, for which our people die.
Twelve miles of road we've made, a little only,
Westward winding. Of human blood and stone
We build; and in a thousand years will come
Beyond the hills to sea."

                I went with them,
Taking a lantern, which upon their faces
Showed years and grief; and in a time we came
To the wild road which wound among wild hills
Westward; and so along this road we stopped,
Silent, thinking of all the dead men, there
Compounded with sad clay. Slowly we moved:
For they were old and weak, had given all
Their life, to build this twelve poor miles of road,
Muddy, under the rain. And in my hand
Turning the lantern, here or there, I saw
Deep holes of water where the raindrop splashed,
And rainfilled footprints in the grass, and heaps
Of broken stone, and rusted spades and picks,
And helves of axes. And the old man spoke,
Holding my wrist: "Three hundred years it took
To build these miles of road: three hundred years;
And human lives unnumbered. But the day
Will come when it is done." Then spoke another,

One not so old, but old, whose face was wrinkled:
"And when it comes, our people will all sing
For joy, passing from east to west, or west
To east, returning, with the light behind them;
All meeting in the road and singing there."
And the third said: "The road will be their life;
A heritage of blood. Grief will be in it,
And beauty out of grief. And I can see
How all the women's faces will be bright.
In that time, laughing, they will remember us.
Blow out your lantern now, for day is coming."

My lantern blown out, in a little while
We climbed in long light up a hill, where climbed
The dwindling road, and ended in a field.
Peasants were working in the field, bowed down
With unrewarded work, and grief, and years
Of pain. And as we passed them, one man fell
Into a furrow that was bright with water
And gave a cry that was half cry, half song—
"The road . . . the road . . . the road . . ." And
    all then fell
Upon their knees and sang.

                We four passed on
Over the hill, to westward. . . . Then I felt
How tears ran down my face, tears without end,
And knew that all my life henceforth was weeping,
Weeping, thinking of human grief, and human
Endeavour fruitless in a world of pain.
And when I held my hands up they were old;
I knew my face would not be young again.

Conrad Aiken

AND IN THE HANGING GARDENS—

AND in the hanging gardens there is rain
From midnight until one, striking the leaves
And bells of flowers, and stroking boles of planes,
And drawing slow arpeggios over pools
And stretching strings of sound from eaves to ferns.
The princess reads. The knave of diamonds sleeps.
The king is drunk, and flings a golden goblet
Down from the turret window (curtained with rain)
Into the lilacs.
          And at one o'clock
The vulcan under the garden wakes and beats
The gong upon his anvil. Then the rain
Ceases, but gently ceases, dripping still,
And sound of falling water fills the dark
As leaves grow bold and upright, and as eaves
Part with water. The princess turns the page
Beside the candle, and between two braids
Of golden hair. And reads: "From there I went
Northward a journey of four days, and came
To a wild village in the hills, where none
Was living save the vulture and the rat
And one old man who laughed but could not speak.
The roofs were fallen in, the well grown over
With weed. And it was here my father died.
Then eight days further, bearing slightly west,
The cold wind blowing sand against our faces,
The food tasting of sand. And as we stood

By the dry rock that marks the highest point
My brother said: 'Not too late is it yet
To turn, remembering home.'   And we were silent
Thinking of home."   The princess shuts her eyes
And feels the tears forming beneath her eyelids
And opens them, and tears fall on the page.
The knave of diamonds in the darkened room
Throws off his covers, sleeps, and snores again.
The king goes slowly down the turret stairs
To find the goblet.

                    And at two o'clock
The vulcan in his smithy underground
Under the hanging gardens, where the drip
Of rain among the clematis and ivy
Still falls from sipping flower to purple flower
Smites twice his anvil, and the murmur comes
Among the roots and vines.   The princess reads:
"As I am sick, and cannot write you more,
And have not long to live, I give this letter
To him, my brother, who will bear it south
And tell you how I died.   Ask how it was,
There in the northern desert, where the grass
Was withered, and the horses, all but one,
Perished . . ."   The princess drops her golden head
Upon the page between her two white arms
And golden braids.   The knave of diamonds wakes
And at his window in the darkened room
Watches the lilacs tossing, where the king
Seeks for the goblet.

                    And at three o'clock

Conrad Aiken

The moon inflames the lilac heads, and thrice
The vulcan, in his root-bound smithy, clangs
His anvil; and the sounds creep softly up
Among the vines and walls. The moon is round,
Round as a shield above the turret top.
The princess blows her candle out, and weeps
In the pale room, where scent of lilacs comes,
Weeping, with hands across her eyelids, thinking
Of withered grass, withered by sandy wind.
The knave of diamonds, in his darkened room,
Holds in his hands a key, and softly steps
Along the corridor, and slides the key
Into the door that guards her. Meanwhile, slowly,
The king, with raindrops on his beard and hands,
And dripping sleeves, climbs up the turret stairs,
Holding the goblet upright in one hand;
And pauses on the midmost step, to taste
One drop of wine, wherewith wild rain has mixed.

Conrad Aiken

SEA HOLLY

BEGOTTEN by the meeting of rock with rock,
The mating of rock and rock, rocks gnashing to-
   gether;
Created so, and yet forgetful, walks
The seaward path, puts up her left hand, shades
Blue eyes, the eyes of rock, to see better
In slanting light the ancient sheep (which kneels
Biting the grass) the while her other hand,
Holding the wicker handle, turns the basket
Of eggs.   The sea is high to-day.   The eggs
Are cheaper.   The sea is blown from the southwest
Confused, taking up sand and mud in waves.
The waves break, sluggish, in brown foam, the wind
Disperses (on the sheep and hawthorn) spray,—
And on her cheeks, the cheeks engendered of rock
And eyes, the colour of rock.   The left hand
Falls from the eyes, and undecided slides
Over the left breast on which muslin lightly
Rests, touching the nipple, and then down
The hollow side, virgin as rock, and bitterly
Caresses the blue hip.
                         It was for this,
This obtuse taking of the seaward path,
This stupid hearing of larks, this hooking
Of wicker, this absent observation of sheep
Kneeling in harsh sea-grass, the cool hand shading
The spray-stung eyes—it was for this the rock
8

Smote itself. The sea is higher to-day,
And eggs are cheaper. The eyes of rock take in
The seaward path that winds toward the sea,
The thistle-prodder, old woman under a bonnet,
Forking the thistles, her back against the sea,
Pausing, with hard hands on the handle, peering
With rock-eyes from her bonnet.
                              It was for this,
This rock-lipped facing of brown waves, half sand
And half water, this tentative hand that slides
Over the breast of rock, and into the hollow
Soft side of muslin rock, and then fiercely
Almost as rock against the hip of rock—
It was for this in midnight the rocks met,
And dithered together, cracking and smoking.
                              It was for this,
Barren beauty, barrenness of rock that aches
On the seaward path, seeing the fruitful sea,
Hearing the lark of rock that sings, smelling
The rock-flower of hawthorn, sweetness of rock,—
It was for this, stone-pain in the stony heart,
The rock loved and laboured; and all is lost.

Conrad Aiken

PSYCHOMACHIA

TENT-CATERPILLARS, as you see (he said)
Have nested in these cherry-trees, and stripped
All sound of leaves from them. You see their webs
Like broken harp-strings, of a fairy kind,
Shine in the moonlight.

              And then I to him:
But is this why, when all the houses sleep,
You meet me here—to tell me only this,
That caterpillars weave their webs in trees?
This road I know. I have walked many times
These sandy ruts. I know these starveling trees—
Their gesture of stiff agony in winter,
And the sharp conscious pain that gnaws them now.
But there is mystery, a message learned,
A word flung down from nowhere, caught by you,
And hither brought for me. How shines that word,
From what star comes it? . . . This is what I seek.

And he in answer: Can you hear the blood
Cry out like jangled bells from all these twigs?
Or feel the ghosts of blossom touch your face?
Walk you amid these trees as one who walks
Upon a field where lie the newly slain
And those who darkly die? And hear you crying?
Flesh here is torn from flesh. The tongue's plucked
    out.

10

What speech then would you have, where speech is
    tongueless,
And nothing, nothing, but a welling up of pain?

I answered: you may say these smitten trees
Being leafless have no tongues and cannot speak.
How comforts that my question? . . . You have
    come,
I know, as you come always, with a meaning.
What, then, is in your darkness of hurt trees;
What bird, sequestered in that wilderness
Of inarticulate pain, wrong ill-endured,
And death not understood, but bides his time
To sing a piercing phrase? Why sings he not?
I am familiar, long, with pain and death,
Endure, as all do, lift dumb eyes to question
Uncomprehended wounds; I have my forest
Of injured trees, whose bare twigs show the moon
Their shameful floating webs; and I have walked,
As now we walk, to listen there to bells
Of pain, bubbles of blood, and ached to feel
The ghosts of blossom pass. But is there not
The mystery, the fugitive shape that sings
A sudden beauty there that comes like peace?

You know this road, he said, and how it leads
Beyond starved trees to bare grey poverty grass;
Then lies the marsh beyond, and then the beach,
With dry curled waves of sea-weed, and the sea.
There, in the fog, you hear the row-locks thump;

11

And there you've seen the fisherman come in,
From insubstantial nothing, to a shore
As dim and insubstantial. He is old,
His boat is old and grey, the oars are worn.
You know this?   You have seen this?

                          And then I:
I know, have seen this, and have felt the shore
As dim and thin as mist; and I have wondered
That it upheld me, did not let me fall
Through nothing into nothing. . . . And the oars,
Worn down like human nerves against the world;
And the worn road that leads to sleeping houses
And weeping trees.   But is this all you say?
For there is mystery, a word you have
That shines within your mind.   Now speak that
    word!

And he in answer: So you have the landscape
With all its nerves and voices.   It is yours.
Do with it what you will.   But never try
To go away from it, for that is death.
Dwell in it, know its houses and cursed trees,
And call it sorrow.   Is this not enough?
Love you not shameful webs?   It is enough.
There is no need for bird, or sudden peace.

II

The plain no herbage had, but all was bare
And swollen livid sand in ridges heaped,

And in the sharp cold light that filled the east
Beneath one cloud that was a bird with wings
I saw a figure shape itself, as whirling
It took up sand and moved across the sand.
A man it was, and here and there he ran
Beating his arms, now falling, rising now,
Struggling, for so it seemed, against the air.
But as I watched, the cloud that was a bird
Lifted its wings, and the white light intense
Poured down upon him. Then I saw him,.naked,
Amid that waste at war with a strange beast
Or monster, many-armed and ever-changing,
That now was like an octopus of air
Now like a spider with a woman's hair
And woman's hands, and now was like a vine
That wrapped him round with leaves and sudden
    flowers,
And now was like a huge white thistledown
Floating; and with this changing shape he fought
Furious and exhausted, till at length
I saw him fall upon it on the sand
And strangle it. Its tentacles of leaves
Fell weakly downward from his back, its flowers
Turned black. And then as he had whirled at first,
So whirled he now again, and with his feet
Drew out the sand, and made a pit, and flung
The scorpion-woman-vine therein; and heaped
The sand above.
        And then I heard him sing
And saw him dance; and all that swollen plain

Where no herb grew became a paradise
Of flowers, and smoking grass, and blowing trees
That shook out birds and song of birds. And he
In power and beauty shining like a demon
Danced there, until that cloud that was a bird
Let fall its wings and darkened him, and hid
The shining fields. But still for long I heard
His voice, and bird-song bells about him chiming,
And knew him dancing there above that grave.

III

Said he: Thus draw your secret sorrow forth,
Whether it wear a woman's face or not;
Walk there at dusk beside that grove of trees,
And sing, and she will come. For while she haunts
Your shameful wood with all its webs and wounds
And darkly broods and works her mischief there,
No peace you'll have, but snares and poisonous
    flowers
And trees in lamentation. Call her out
As memory cries the white ghost from the tomb.
Play the sharp lyric flute, for that she loves,
With topaz phrases for her vanity.

And I in answer: She is dear to me,
Dearer that in my mind she makes a dark
Of woods and rocks and thorns and venomous
    flowers.
What matter that I seldom see her face,

14

Or have her beauty never? She is there,
It is her voice I hear in cries of trees.
This may be misery, but it is blest.

Then he: And when you have her, strongly take
Her protean fiery body and lithe arms
And wailing mouth and growing vines of hair
And leaves that turn to hands, and bear her forth
Into that landscape that is rightly yours
And dig a grave for her and thrust her in
All writhing, and so cover her with earth.
Then will the two, as should be, fuse in one.
The landscape, that was dead, will straightway
    shine
And sing and flower about you, trees will grow
Where desert was, water will flash from dust,
And rocks grow out in leaves. And you, this grief
Torn from your heart and planted in your world,
Will know yourself at peace.

                    But will it be—
I asked—as bright a joy to see that landscape
Put on diffused her wonder, sing her name,
Burn with the vital secret of her body
There locked in earth like fire, as now to have
Her single beauty fugitive in my mind?
If she is lost, will flowering rocks give peace?

And he in answer: So you have the landscape
With all her nerves and voices. She is yours.

Conrad Aiken

THE WEDDING

At noon, Tithonus, withered by his singing,
Climbing the oatstalk with his hairy legs,
Met grey Arachne, poisoned and shrunk down
By her own beauty; pride had shrivelled both.
In the white web—where seven flies hung wrapped—
She heard his footstep; hurried to him; bound him;
Enshrouded him in silk; then poisoned him.
Twice shrieked Tithonus, feebly; then was still.
Arachne loved him.   Did he love Arachne?
She watched him with red eyes, venomous sparks,
And the furred claws outspread. . . . "O sweet
    Tithonus!
Darling!   Be kind, and sing that song again!
Shake the bright web again with that deep fiddling!
Are you much poisoned? sleeping? do you dream?
Darling Tithonus!"
               And Tithonus, weakly
Moving one hairy shin against the other
Within his silken sack, contrived to fiddle
A little tune, half-hearted: "Shrewd Arachne!
Whom pride in beauty withered to this shape
As pride in singing shrivelled me to mine—
Unwrap me, let me go—and let me limp,
With what poor strength your venom leaves me,
    down
This oatstalk, and away."
              Arachne, angry,

Stung him again, twirling him with rough paws,
The red eyes keen. "What! You would dare to
    leave me?
Unkind Tithonus! Sooner I'll kill and eat you
Than let you go. But sing that tune again—
So plaintive was it!"
                 And Tithonus faintly
Moved the poor fiddles, which were growing cold,
And sang: "Arachne, goddess envied of gods,
Beauty's eclipse eclipsed by angry beauty,
Have pity, do not ask the withered heart
To sing too long for you! My strength goes out,
Too late we meet for love. Oh, be content
With friendship, which the noon sun once may
    kindle
To give one flash of passion like a dewdrop,
Before it goes. . . . Be reasonable,—Arachne!"

Arachne heard the song grow weaker, dwindle
To first a rustle, and then half a rustle,
And last a tick, so small no ear could hear it
Save hers, a spider's ear. And her small heart
(Rusted away, like his, to a pinch of dust)
Gleamed once, like his, and died. She clasped him
    tightly
And sunk her fangs in him. Tithonus dead,
She slept awhile, her last sensation gone;
Woke from the nap, forgetting him; and ate him.

Conrad Aiken

POVERTY GRASS

FIRST, blow the trumpets!   Call the people hither!
Set hornsmen at all crossroads: send out horsemen
With horns, a man's length, bound in brass,
Far to the north, the west.   Bid them to blow
Unceasing summons, shatter the air, shake leaves
From trees decrepit.   I would have the world
Sound with a bugle music from end to end.
Lead then the people hither, have the roads
Black with the mass of them at night and noon.
And when you have them, see them banked about me,
Row behind row—(how shine already the faces!)—
Like angels in Angelico's dream of heaven.
Those that were horsemen first will now be ushers—
"Stand here!" they'll cry, "no crowding!—Those
        behind
Will hear, feel, understand, as well as those
Who rest their chins upon him, prop their elbows
Against the coffin-lid.   Stand still! be patient."
As for the house—that must be fit as well.
Thus, as it now stands—no! it is too meagre.
The stage is bare. . . . First, the approach is bad.
The hill, behind, that for a thousand years
Has washed its loam and leaves down in the rains,
Against these walls—(enough, all seen at once,
To whelm the roof, not leave the chimney, even)—
The hill must go. . . . So, let a thousand axes
Flash against bark: let fall a thousand oaks

With all their crying birds, small scolding squirrels,
Bees' nests and birds' nests, hornets, wasps, and
    snakes.
A thousand carts, each with a quaking tree
Outstretched in ignominy, chained and helpless,—
These, going hence, will be our first procession:
We'll bear to the sea our captives. Next, an army
With spades and picks a thousand, have them led
To music, up the hill, and then like ants
Devour him: gash him first, and swarm in the gash,
Eat inward till he's maggoty with men,—
A hollow seething shell,—and lastly, nothing.
As for the house, its walls must be of glass.
And no partitions! one vast room that's walled
And roofed with clearest crystal. There at night
We'll have great light, ten thousand flames of can-
    dles,
Ten thousand clear-eyed flames in a crystal casket:
The folk on the utmost hill will see, and cry
"Look, how the moon's caught in a crystal coffin!"
And last, myself, there in that crystal coffin,
Flooded with light, reclining half, half sitting
Propped up amid soft silks in a little box
Of brilliant glass, yet lidless. There I'll sit
Like prophet at a tomb's edge, open-mouthed,
Pale, old, obscene, white-bearded—see! my beard
Hangs on the coffin as a snow-drift hangs
On a wall of ice. . . . And there, at last, I'll speak.

So, then! You see it clearly. It is night-time.

Conrad Aiken

The house is bright. And I,—in an open coffin,—
(That, too, in the coffin that we call the world,
Large, airy, lucent, lighted with lights of stars,—)
Peer from the luminous grave's edge into darkness
That's filled from hub to marge with staring faces.
Beautiful! Is the world here? Let it gaze, then,
And fill its idiot eyes to overflowing
With a sight not known before. Step closer, kings,—
Emperors, use your elbows as the plebs do.
Steam, if you like, with your ambitious breath
These walls that tell no lies. I'd have you hear me,
You most of all; though I forget not either
The vast grey hungry maggot-mass of men:
The little wedge-shaped darlings, in their broth
Of carrion illusions! . . . How they rot
The air they breathe, turn the green earth to poison,
People the sky with pestilence of sick fancies!
See how the whole sky swarms with dirty wings!

O Man! who so corrupt all things you feed on;
Whose meditation slimes the thing it thinks;
Vile borer into the core of the universe;
Spoiler and destroyer; you, ambitious,
Crawling upon your admirable belly
For nothing but that at last your tube-shaped mouth
Should blindly suck and thrust at the innermost
    heart
Of the world, or god, or infinite overthrown;
Foulest and most dishonest of all creatures;
Sole traitorous worm of all things living, you
20

Conrad Aiken

Who crown your horrible head with a dream of glory
And call yourself a king!   Come closer, hear me,
I am the prophet who, as through these walls
Of innocent glass, see all things deep and clear,
The after and before, revealed or hid:
Partly among you living, partly dead,
I see your hungry mouths, but also see
With my dead eye,—(one cold eye underground
Beneath the earth's black coffin-lid),—the dead.
Ha!   You would have my secret?   You would hear
The one bright shattering trumpet, whose long blast
Blows like a whirlwind myriad ghosts from tombs?
You cry to the prophet, do you, for a vision—
You'd have me, with one sombre word of magic,
Cry beauty back from dust, and set to singing
This catacomb of graves you call a world? . . .
Press closer, kings!   Swarm over me, you plebs!
Feed your rapacious eyes on me, devour
With mouths and nerves and nostrils and raw brains
This bloodless carcase that contains your secret:
Have out my heart, hold up above it candles,
Pass it among you, squeak and growl and jabber,
Stamp it beneath your feet—it's an old leaf
Will turn to a little dust. . . . For there's the won-
      der.
I am but poverty grass; a dry grey weed;
A trifling dusty moss fine-branched as coral;
One footstep makes it powder.   And my secret,
Which all my hornsmen brought you here to learn,
Is nought but this: this singing world of yours

Is but a heap of bones. Sound once the trumpet
And you shall see them, tier upon tier, profound
As god himself. Sound twice the trumpet, then,
And I will add my bone or two. And after,
At the third blast, will all these lights puff out,
And you may grope in darkness, as you came.
Sound the bright horn! Shut, coffin! I am dead.

Conrad Aiken

GOD'S ACRE

In Memory of. In Fondest Recollection
Of. In Loving Memory of. . . . In Fond
Remembrance. Died in October. Died at Sea.
Who died at sea? The name of the seaport
Escapes her, gone, blown with the eastwind, over
The tombs and yews, into the apple orchard;
Over the road—where gleams a wagon-top—
And gone. The eastwind gallops up from sea
Bringing salt and gulls. The marsh smell, too,
Strong in September; mud and reeds, the reeds
Rattling like bones.
                She shifts the grass-clipper
From right to left hand, clips and clips the grass.
The broken column, carefully broken, on which
The blackbird hen is laughing—in fondest memory.
Burdon! Who was this Burdon, to be remembered?
Or Potter? The Potter rejected by the pot.
"Here lies Josephus Burdon, who departed
This life the fourth of August, ninteen hundred.
'And He said Come.' " Josephus Burdon, forty,
Gross, ribald, with strong hands on which was hair,
And red ears kinked with hair, and northblue eyes,
Held in one hand a hammer, in the other
A nail. He drove the nail. . . . This was enough?
Or—(also)—did he love? . . .
                . . . She changes back
The clipper. The blades are dull. The grass is wet,

23

And gums the blades. In Loving Recollection.
The chains, heavy, hang round the vault. What
    chance
For skeletons? The dead men rise at night,
Rattle the links. "Too heavy! can't be budged. . . .
Try once again together— Now! . . . No use."
They sit in moonless shadow, gently talking.
"Old Jones it must have been who made those
    chains!
I'd like to see him lift them now!" . . . The owl
That hunts in Wickham Wood comes over, mewing.
"An owl," says one. "Most likely," says another.
They turn grey heads.

            The seawind brings a breaking
Bellsound among the yews and tombstones, flinging
The twisted whorls of bronze on sunlit stones.
Sacred . . . memory . . . affectionate. . . . O God,
What travesty is this?—the blackbird soils
The broken column; the worm at work in the skull
Feasts on medulla; and the lewd thrush cracks
A snailshell on the vault. He died on shipboard.
Seaburial, then, were better?

                    On her knees
She clips and clips, kneeling against the sod,
Gripping the world between her two knees, ponder-
    ing
Downward, as though her thought, like men or
    apples,
Fell downward into earth. Seablue, her eyes
Turn to the sea. Seagulls are scavengers,

Conrad Aiken

Cruel of face, but lovely. By the dyke
The reeds rattle, leaping in eastwind, rattling
Like bones. In Fond Rememberance Of. O God
That life is what it is and does not change.
You there in earth and I above you kneeling.
You dead, and I alive.

                  She prods a plantain
Of too ambitious root. That largest yewtree
Clutching the hill—

              She rises from stiff knees,
Stiffly, and treads the pebble path, that leads
Downward to sea and town. The marsh smell
    comes
Healthy and salt and fills her nostrils. Reeds
Dance in the eastwind, rattling; warblers dart
Flashing from swaying reed to reed, and sing.

Conrad Aiken

THE ROOM

THROUGH that window—all else being extinct
Except itself and me—I saw the struggle
Of darkness against darkness. Within the room
It turned and turned, dived downward. Then I saw
How order might—if chaos wished—become:
And saw the darkness crush upon itself,
Contracting powerfully; it was as if
It killed itself, slowly: and with much pain.
Pain. The scene was pain, and nothing but pain.
What else, when chaos draws all forces inward
To shape a single leaf? . . .

                    For the leaf came
Alone and shining in the empty room;
After a while the twig shot downward from it;
And from the twig a bough; and then the trunk,
Massive and coarse; and last the one black root.
The black root cracked the walls. Boughs burst the
      window:
The great tree took possession.

                    Tree of trees!
Remember (when time comes) how chaos died
To shape the shining leaf. Then turn, have courage,
Wrap arms and roots together, be convulsed
With grief, and bring back chaos out of shape.
I will be watching then as I watch now.
I will praise darkness now, but then the leaf.

WILLIAM ROSE BENET

William Rose Benet

WHALE

Rain, with a silver flail;
Sun, with a golden ball;
Ocean, wherein the whale
Swims minnow-small;

I heard the whale rejoice
And cynic sharks attend;
He cried with a purple voice,
"The Lord is my Friend!"

" 'With flanged and battering tail,
With huge and dark baleen,'
He said, 'Let there be Whale
In the Cold and Green!'

"He gave me a water spout,
A side like a harbor wall;
The Lord from cloud looked out
And planned it all!

"With glittering crown atilt
He leaned on a glittering rail;
He said, 'Where Sky is spilt
Let there be Whale!'

"Tier upon tier of wings
Blushed and blanched and bowed,

Phalanxed fiery things
Cried in the cloud;

"Million-eyed was the mirk
At the plan not understood;
But the Lord looked on his work
And saw it was good.

"He gave me marvelous girth
For the curve of back and breast
And a tiny eye of mirth
To hide his jest;

"He made me a floating hill,
A plunging deep-sea mine.
This was the Lord's will,
The Lord is divine!

"I magnify his name
In earthquake and eclipse,
In weltering molten flame
And wrecks of ships,

"In waves that lick the moon,—
I, the plough of the sea;
I am the Lord's boon,
The Lord made me!"

The sharks barked from beneath,
As the great whale rollicked and roared,

"Yes, and our grinning teeth,—
Was it not the Lord!"

Then question pattered like hail
From fishes large and small.
"The Lord is mighty," said Whale,
"The Lord made all!

"His is a mammoth jest
Life may never betray.
He has laid it up in his breast
Till Judgment Day.

"But high when combers foam
And tower their last of all,
My power shall haul you home
Through Heaven wall.

"A trumpet then in the gates,
To the ramps a thundering drum,
I shall lead you where He waits
For his Whale to come.

"Where his cloudy seat is placed
On high in the empty dome
I shall trail the Ocean abased
In chains of foam,

"Unwieldy, squattering dread.
Where the blazing cohorts stand

31

William Rose Benet

At last I shall lift my head
As it feels his hand.

"Then wings with a million eyes
Before mine eyes shall quail.
'Look you, all Paradise,
I was his Whale!' "

I heard the Whale rejoice
As he splayed the waves to a fan.
"And the Lord shall say with his Voice,
'Leviathan!'

"The Lord shall say with his Tongue,
'Now let all Heaven give hail
To my jest when I was young,
To my very Whale!' "

Then the Whale careened in the sea,
He floundered with flailing tail
Flourished and rollicked he,
"Aha, mine Empery!
For the Lord said, 'Let Whale be!'
And There Was Whale!"

William Rose Benet

ROGUES' APOCALYPSE

"THE DEVIL'S DEN" was the bousing-ken
Of Tom-o'-Bedlam and his Abram men.
Cutpurse, cogger and Egyptian swart
Banged leaden tankards, held high court.
With whey-white faces, patched and scarred,
Rogues of all races, evil-starred,
Wet their whistles, thumped with their sticks,
Brandished the crutch like a crucifix.

Softly sifted the goose-feather snow
From plum-blue night to the Town below,
On crooked streets cobbled, on red roofs peaked.
Where shutters clacked and a sign-board creaked,
Where wavered and fell a golden splotch
From the passing lanterns of the watch,
Rug-gowned halberdiers searching for the
Moon-men painted Moorish-swarthy.

The Gypsies' jackman, bold Jack Kettle,
Bounced from his seat on the firelit settle.
"The gift of a tongue, to all 'tis given,
So up, bully boys, in a song of Heaven!"
And "Heaven!" that mort of wild rogues roared
As leaden tankards crashed on the board,
"A song of Heaven—and set to an air
For the ballad-singers of Stourbridge Fair!"

Bawled Pitch, the pirate, straight from Devon,
"Aye, clapper-dudgeons, a song o' Heaven!"
"Some jack o' the clock-house," shrieked Meg the
    Harlot,
"Shall write it after in gold and scarlet!"
And a tinker, hung with his pewter dishes,
Crack-brained, cackled of "loaves and fishes,"
When in through the door on their sudden gabble
Floated a music that stilled the rabble:

First
Some harp
Like a sword blade sharp
Clove through azure ether
With an edge like fire;
Then
A horn
In a harsh gold scorn
Trumpeted rebellion over wind and wire;

High over towers and gray walls graven
The sun was a lion that ramped through heaven;
Deep under jasper cliffs where it curled
The mist was a snake that swallowed the world!

Wilder the minstrelsy swelled and gayer.
Bright in the door, like a strolling player,
Stood a man in a cloak like four-fold wings—
Flickering fingers on flickering strings.
Then, as though at a "Silver ram! trim-tram—

Pass—presto!" the walls of the building swam
To mist.   They were 'ware all around him there
Of a glittering crowd in the blue night air:

Raphael, Michael and Gabriel,
Uriel and Jeremiel,
Nephelim of the sons of Seth,
(Pharaoh's children caught their breath!)
Rank on rank of the troops that trod
Where Jacob visioned the camps of God,
Mentors of David and Elias,
Guides to Daniel and Zacharias!

Around them thrilled that Voice of wonders
That spake to John as with seven thunders
From their lips went forth the troublous word
That Daniel in Shushan's palace heard;
Like clean wool flowed their straight attire;
Like burnished brass, like a silver fire
Their beauty blazed that consumed earth's daugh-
        ters;
"The noise of their wings was the noise of waters."

All crouched and quaked at the shine and burning,
At the roar as of wheels within wheels turning.
Then Night came clap; that wild event
In glittering rose through the firmament,
Upward streamed through a crystal heaven
The inner cordon, the Mystic Seven,
Their wingèd cohorts whirling, whitening . . .
From the wintry sky there went forth lightning!

35

William Rose Benet

Jack Kettle gaped.   He was long past speaking.
From Tib the Tinker came rabbit-squeaking.
Though Pitch had fought blood-slippery decks, he
Wallowed now in an apoplexy;
But Meg stood forth where all fell prone:
"In the likeness of a sapphire stone . . ."
She whispered.   "I see the darkness riven;
He comes with power in the clouds of Heaven!"

And afar
A harp
Like a sword blade sharp
Clove the azure ether
With a burning strain;
On high
Some horn
In a silver scorn
Rang for resurrection from the pit of pain . . .

The echoes ended.   The dawn's faint rose
Slowly crept over ghostly snows.

William Rose Benet

THE FAWN IN THE SNOW

THE brown-dappled fawn
Bereft of the doe
Shivers in blue shadow
Of the glaring snow,

His whole world bright
As a jewel, and hard,
Diamond white,
Turquoise barred.

The trees are black,
Their needles gold,
Their boughs crack
In the keen cold.

The brown-dappled fawn
Bereft of the doe
Trembles and shudders
At the bright snow.

The air whets
The warm throat,
The frost frets
At the smooth coat.

Brown agate eyes
Opened round

Agonize
At the cold ground,

At the cold heaven
Enamelled pale,
At the earth shriven
By the snowy gale,

At magic glitter
Burning to blind,
At beauty bitter
As an almond rind.

Fawn, fawn,
Seek for your south,
For kind dawn
With her cool mouth,

For green sod
With gold and blue
Dappled, as God
Has dappled you,

For slumbrous ease,
Firm turf to run
Through fruited trees
Into full sun!

The shivering fawn
Paws at the snow.

William Rose Benet

South and dawn
Lie below;

Richness and mirth,
Dearth forgiven,
A happy earth,
A warm heaven,

The sleet streams,
The snow flies;
The fawn dreams
With wide brown eyes.

William Rose Benet

MOON RIDER

A sky of deepening bronze
Seemed tolling like a bell.
Blue ice filmed shrivelled ponds.
Snow whispering fell.

Trees traced a frieze of black.
One window's spark
Flecked gold upon the farmyard track,
Brightening with the dark.

He cinched the saddle on the colt
That snuffed his hand.
The bar was slid, the bolt
Shot. The open land

Lay ghostly still from hill to hill.
He sprang. They were gone.
Like foam below them tossed the snow.
Hoofs beat on.

Blurred in the eyes like unshed tears
Stars crackled overhead;
The wind a flickering shears
That snaps a thread.

Swift between drifts the flooding thud
Ran muffled on.

William Rose Benet

Straight at the moon he rode
In goblin dawn.

Dark trees to one high house
Closed round him up the drive.
He reined in hush that seemed to rouse
The voice of all alive.

Pebbles that, spattering, ticked the glass
Awoke a crocus stain.
He saw her shadow pass
The blinded pane.

Over the snow-choked portico
The house leaned heavy-beamed.
A footfall light, a footfall low.
The fanlight gleamed.

Cautious, the oak both groaned and spoke.
One golden bud of flame.
Shadows tall thronged from the hall.
Name breathed to name.

In frosted heaven the moon's shell
Filled, overflowed with light,
Welling like ringing of a bell
Through the lingering night.

STAGE DIRECTIONS

TRUMPETS. Enter a King, in the sunset glare.
He sits in an antique chair. He fingers an antique
ring.
The heavy cloak on his back is gold and black.

The hall is tall with gloom. A window stands
Full of scarlet sky. The hands of trees entreat the
room,
Plucking and plucking the pane. An oblong stain

Of scarlet is flat on the floor. The projected flare
Slants to the foot of the chair. The chamber's
farther door
Slowly advances its edge. A smoky wedge

Of thick blue mist, growing wider as the door
swings
Noiseless, twitches the king's hands. He is crouched
like a spider.
His eyes are green as glass. Shudderings pass

That shrink him deep in his cloak. The door is
wide.
The doorway, from side to side, is packed with mist
like smoke.
The dreadful scarlet dies from the windowed skies.

William Rose Benet

Silence crosses the room. Nothing more.
Silence crowds from the door, gathers, gathers in
   gloom.
His fluttering fingers rise to cover his eyes.

Silence says nothing at all. It is thickly pressed,
Like a multitude obsessed with terror, from wall to
   wall.
Silence, deep with dread, is the weight of lead

That slowly constricts his breast. Fingers fight
At the throat, in fierce despite of death, as the
   drowned resist
Green gulfs that roar and ring. . . .

Exit the King.

William Rose Benet

FIRE AND GLASS

THE thistly yellow flame flows up like water,
  The dusk brick glows.
Fashion the rope-like glass; your lip can blow it
  To a vase like a rose,   [a lily.
To a goblet curved like a wave, with a stem like
  Glass can be spun
To frailer lace than the cobweb brown old spiders
  Weave in the sun.

Not pure gold ingots nor all the renown of iron
  Nor the blushing brand,
Nor crackling cataracts of molten metal
  Kissing the sand,
So praise this cleanly and bewildered fury
  Potent to shape
Emerging contours scintillant as diamond,
  Smooth as the grape.

O self-consuming sun, the dew-on-the-gossamer's
  Delicate glint,   [as flowers
What symmetries petalled and pearled and fragile
  Take form and tint
From this fierce unslakable thirst and famine of fire
  Cold stars control!   [rebellion,—
Even thus, O love, through the blood's rebuked
  Thus my soul—!

William Rose Benet

JESSE JAMES

(A Design in Red and Yellow for a Nickel Library.)

JESSE JAMES was a two-gun man,
     (Roll on, Missouri!)
Strong-arm chief of an outlaw clan.
     (From Kansas to Illinois!)
He twirled an old Colt forty-five;
     (Roll on, Missouri!)
They never took Jesse James alive.
     (Roll, Missouri, roll!)

Jesse James was King of the Wes';
     (Cataracks in the Missouri!)
He'd a di'mon' heart in his lef' breas';
     (Brown Missouri rolls!)
He'd a fire in his heart no hurt could stifle;
     (Thunder, Missouri!)
Lion eyes an' a Winchester rifle.
     (Missouri, roll down!)

Jesse James rode a pinto hawse;
Come at night to a water-cawse;
Tetched with the rowel that pinto's flank;
She sprung the torrent from bank to bank.

Jesse rode through a sleepin' town;
Looked the moonlit street both up an' down;

45

William Rose Benet

Crack-crack-crack, the street ran flames
An' a great voice cried, "I'm Jesse James!"

Hawse an' afoot they're after Jess!
  (*Roll on, Missouri!*)
Spurrin' an' spurrin'—but he's gone Wes'.
  (*Brown Missouri rolls!*)
He was ten foot tall when he stood in his boots;
  (*Lightnin' light the Missouri!*)
More'n a match fer sich galoots.
  (*Roll, Missouri, roll!*)

Jesse James rode outa the sage;
Roun' the rocks come the swayin' stage;
Straddlin' the road a giant stan's
An' a great voice bellers, "Throw up yer han's!"

Jesse raked in the di'mon' rings,
The big gold watches an' the yuther things;
Jesse divvied 'em then an' thar
With a cryin' child had lost her mar.

The U. S. troopers is after Jess;
  (*Roll on, Missouri!*)
Their hawses sweat foam, but he's gone Wes';
  (*Hear Missouri roar!*)
He was broad as a b'ar, he'd a ches' like a drum,
  (*Wind an' rain through Missouri!*)
An' his red hair flamed like Kingdom Come.
  (*Missouri down to the sea!*)

46

William Rose Benet

Jesse James all alone in the rain
Stopped an' stuck up the Eas'-boun' train;
Swayed through the coaches with horns an' a
tail,
Lit out with the bullion an' the registered mail.

Jess made 'em all turn green with fright
Quakin' in the aisles in the pitch-black night;
An' he give all the bullion to a pore ole tramp
Campin' nigh the cuttin' in the dirt an' damp.

The whole U. S. is after Jess;
    (*Roll on, Missouri!*)
The son-of-a-gun, if he ain't gone Wes';
    (*Missouri to the sea!*)
He could chaw cold iron an' spit blue flame;
    (*Cataracks down the Missouri!*)
He rode on a catamount he'd larned to tame.
    (*Hear that Missouri roll!*)

Jesse James rode into a bank;
Give his pinto a tetch on the flank;
Jumped the teller's window with an awful crash;
Heaved up the safe an' twirled his mustache;

He said, "So long, boys!" He yelped, "So long!
Feelin' porely today—I ain't feelin' strong!"
Rode right through the wall a-goin' crack-crack-
crack—
Took the safe home to mother in a gunny-sack.

William Rose Benet

They're creepin', they're crawlin', they're stalkin'
    Jess;
    (*Roll on, Missouri!*)
They's a rumor he's gone much further Wes';
    (*Roll, Missouri, roll!*)
They's word of a cayuse hitched to the bars
    (*Ruddy clouds on Missouri!*)
Of a golden sunset that busts into stars.
    (*Missouri, roll down!*)

Jesse James rode hell fer leather;
He was a hawse an' a man together;
In a cave in a mountain high up in air
He lived with a rattlesnake, a wolf, an' a bear.

Jesse's heart was as sof' as a woman;
Fer guts an' stren'th he was sooper-human;
He could put six shots through a woodpecker's
    eye
And take in one swaller a gallon o' rye.

They sought him here an' they sought him there,
    (*Roll on, Missouri!*)
But he strides by night through the ways of the air;
    (*Brown Missouri rolls!*)
They say he was took an' they say he is dead,
    (*Thunder, Missouri!*)
But he ain't—he's a sunset overhead!
    (*Missouri down to the sea!*)

William Rose Benet

Jesse James was a Hercules.
When he went through the woods he tore up the
trees.
When he went on the plains he smoked the groun'
An' the hull lan' shuddered fer miles aroun'.

Jesse James wore a red bandanner
That waved on the breeze like the Star Spangled
Banner;
In seven states he cut up dadoes.
He's gone with the buffler an' the desperadoes.

Yes, Jesse James was a two-gun man
     (*Roll on, Missouri!*)
The same as when this song began;
     (*From Kansas to Illinois!*)
An' when you see a sunset bust into flames
     (*Lightnin' light the Missouri!*)
Or a thunderstorm blaze—that's Jesse James!
     (*Hear that Missouri roll!*)

H. D.

H. D.

SONGS FROM CYPRUS

I

GATHER for festival
bright weed and purple shell;
make on the holy sand
pattern as one might make
who tread with rose-red heel
a measure
pleasureful;

such as those songs we made
in rose and myrtle shade
where rose and myrtle fell
(shell-petal or rose-shell,)
on just such holy sand;
ah, the song
musical;

give me white rose and red,
find me in citron glade
citron of precious weight,
spread gold before her feet,
ah, weave the citron flower;
hail goddess
beautiful.

H. D.

WHITE rose, O white,
white rose and honey-coloured,
tell me again,
tell me the thing she whispered;

red rose, O wine
fragrant, O subtly flavoured,
cyclamen stain,
how, how has your fire differed

from rose so white?
swift, swift, O Eros-favoured,
part, meet, part—then
rose, be rose-white, unsevered.

H. D.

BRING flutéd asphodel,
take strip and bar of silver,
fling them before Love's shrine;

see the white flowers turn red,
fragrance whereof the dead
breathe faintly by their river,

by Lethe's bank are rose,
and all the silver bars
shape to taut bows and arrows,

wherewith Love fronts his foes,
(ah, friend, beware his quiver)
wherewith Love fronts his foes.

IV

WHERE is the nightingale,
in what myrrh-wood and dim?
ah, let the night come black,
for we would conjure back
all that enchanted him,
  all that enchanted him.

Where is the bird of fire?
in what packed hedge of rose?
in what roofed ledge of flower?
no other creature knows
what magic lurks within,
  what magic lurks within.

Bird, bird, bird, bird, we cry,
hear, pity us in pain:
hearts break in the sunlight,
hearts break in daylight rain,
only night heals again,
  only night heals again.

H. D.

Bring myrrh and myrtle bud,
bell of the snowy head
of the first asphodel;

frost of the citron flower,
petal on petal, white
wax of faint love-delight;

flower, flower and little head
of tiny meadow-floret,
white, where no bee has fed;

full of its honey yet
spilling its scented sweet;
spread them before her feet;

white citron, whitest rose,
(myrrh leaves, myrrh leaves enclose,)
and the white violet.

H. D.

LET ZEUS RECORD

I

I say I am quite done,
quite done with this,
you smile your calm
inveterate chill smile

and light steps back;
intolerate loveliness
smites at the ranks
of obdurate bitterness;

you smile with keen
chiseled and frigid lips;
it seems no evil
ever could have been;

so, on the Parthenon,
like splendour keeps
peril at bay
facing inviolate dawn.

H. D.

MEN cannot mar you,
women cannot break
your innate strength,
your stark autocracy;

still I will make no plea
for this slight verse;
it outlines simply
Love's authority:

but pardon this,
that in these luminous days,
I re-invoke the dark
to frame your praise;

as one to make a bright room
seem more bright,
stares out deliberate
into Cerberus-night.

H. D.

SOMETIMES I chide the manner of your dress;
I want all men to see the grace of you;
I mock your pace, your body's insolence,
thinking that all should praise, while obstinate
you still insist your beauty's gold is clay:

I chide you that you stand not forth entire,
set on bright plinth, intolerably desired;
yet I in turn will cheat, will thwart your whim,
I'll break my thought, weld it to fit your measure,
as one who sets a statue on a height
to show where Hyacinth or Pan have been.

H. D.

WHEN blight lay on the Persian like a scar,
and death was heavy on Athens, plague and war,
you gave me this bright garment and this ring;

I who still kept of wisdom's meagre store
a few rare songs and some philosophising,
offered you these for I had nothing more;

that which both Athens and the Persian mocked
you took, as a cold famished bird takes grain,
blown inland through darkness and withering rain.

H. D.

V

WOULD you prefer myrrh-flower or cyclamen?
I have them, I could spread them out again;
but now for this stark moment while Love breathes
his tentative breath, as dying, yet still lives,
wait as that time you waited tense with me:

others shall love when Athens lives again,
you waited in the agonies of war;
others will praise when all the host proclaims
Athens the perfect; you when Athens lost
stood by her; when the dark perfidious host
turned, it was you who pled for her with death.

H. D.

STARS wheel in purple, yours is not so rare
as Hesperus, nor yet so great a star
as bright Aldebaran or Sirius,
nor yet the stained and brilliant one of War;

stars turn in purple, glorious to the sight;
yours is not gracious as the Pleiads are
nor as Orion's sapphires, luminous;

yet disenchanted, cold, imperious face,
when all the others, blighted, reel and fall,
your star, steel-set, keeps lone and frigid tryst
to freighted ships baffled in wind and blast.

H. D.

NONE watched with me
who watched his fluttering breath,
none brought white roses,
none the roses red;

many had loved,
had sought him luminous,
when he was blithe
and purple draped his bed;

yet when Love fell
struck down with plague and war,
you lay white myrrh-buds
on the darkened lintel;

you fastened blossom
to the smitten sill;
let Zeus record this,
daring Death to mar.

T. S. ELIOT

T. S. Eliot

THREE DREAM SONGS

I

Eyes that last I saw in tears
Through division
Here in death's dream kingdom
The golden vision reappears
I see the eyes but not the tears
This is my affliction.

This is my affliction
Eyes I shall not see again
Eyes of decision
Eyes I shall not see unless
At the door of death's other kingdom
Where, as in this,
The eyes outlast a little while
A little while outlast the tears
And hold us in derision.

T. S. Eliot

II

THE wind sprang up at four o'clock
The wind sprang up and broke the bells
Swinging between life and death
Here, in death's dream kingdom
The waking echo of confusing strife
Is it a dream or something else
When the surface of the blackened river
Is a face that sweats with tears?
I saw across the blackened river
The camp fire shake with alien spears
Here, across death's other river
The Tartar horsemen shake their spears.

T. S. Eliot

III

THIS is the dead land
This is cactus land
Here the stone images
Are raised, here they receive
The supplication of a dead man's hand
Under the twinkle of a fading star.

Is it like this
In death's other kingdom
Waking alone
At the hour when we are
Trembling with tenderness
Lips that would kiss
Form prayers to broken stone.

JOHN GOULD FLETCHER

John Gould Fletcher

LAZARUS

I

LAZARUS wakened, like a drowning man
Drawn from deep water. In the retreating dusk
Gray faces wavered, hollow voices rose,
Strange meaningless syllables of surprise were
    babbled
In an immense void distance, miles away.
They smote across his ears like tingling thunder
And fused to words. He closed his eyes in pain.
Next, on his chest, he felt, as bands of iron,
The grave-clothes still unloosed. Within his mouth
Was leathery thirst, and in his throat cool air
Pulsed in sharp gasping breaths. A whimper rose,
Broke in a sudden sob. He raised aloft
A leaden head and stared. The crowd about him
Grew clearer now. Aloft there was something blue,
With a smudge of green upon it. Trees. The sky.
Drops trickled down his throat and Martha's arms
Encircled him. He closed his eyes again;
And, helpless as a babe unswathed, was drawn
From the tomb-chamber, carried softly home.

II

Days went by slowly; now old thoughts came back
And rearranged themselves about a gap

Of darkness without meaning. He remembered
How, with the fever on him, he had looked,
As now, upon the high wide distant sky,
And heard the pigeons fluttering by the eaves
And cooing on the rooftops. Night and pain
Had sifted down gray ashes; he cried out:
His breath was squeezed from him: and next he saw
The sad gray faces wavering in the dusk
Of the tomb-chamber. What had happened then?
He turned to Martha:—"Martha, was I dead?
Why do I live if I was truly dead?"
But Martha frowned and Mary bit her lip.
He asked again, persisted. Martha said,
"Why do you bother me? You were not dead;
You had enough to kill seven men at least,
Yet came to life the same old good-for-nothing,
Still asking foolish questions. I should think
That fever would have taught you to show sense."
She banged the bread down hard upon the board,
And cowed him into silence. But, that night,
When all was quiet, Mary crept more near:
She whispered, "Go to the city, ask for Simon's
    house,
Seek out the Preacher. He will tell you all;
And maybe give you peace, if there is peace."

III

Here in Jerusalem the gray narrow streets
Smote on his senses like a stifled cry,

74

With stink of bubbling drains, with graybeards
    haggling
Over meat flyblown on an open stall;
Washing hung out to dry, women who stood
In narrow doorways, who, as he passed, drew back
Their robes revealing fat anointed breasts,
With nipples stained with red. Some shops were
    closed
Where Broadway ran to the Procurator's hall,
And not far off was shouting. Lazarus paused
Debating where to go, his brain a jangle,
When round the corner suddenly there swept
A screeching mob into the street and soldiers
Came beating them back with the flat of their heavy
    swords.
Within their midst there walked two men with
    halters
About their necks, and following in their wake,
Half-tottering under the crushing weight
Of a great cross, sweat staining His white robes,
His brows bound 'round with thorns, His pale lips
    twisted
In a fixed smile of agony, walked the Man he
    sought:—
Jesus the Preacher, sprung from Galilee.

IV

Jostled by shoving elbows, with the reek
Of garlicked breaths tainting his nostrils and

With spray of slaver blown into his face,
Stunned by the deafening yells that shook the walls,
Lazarus gasped for breath. As a leaf rolls
Helpless before a gale, battered and torn,
He rolled along with the mob for half-a-minute,
Clutching at coats that shouted, "Here! Get out!"
And the next instant found himself alone,
Safe in an alley. Here an idiot girl
Stood gravely twirling a dirty bit of string
Before him, crooning. Far away the noise
Of shouting dinned and slackened. Through the
    street
One sole belated runner raced to join
The mob. Loud shouted Lazarus after him,
"Where do they carry the Preacher?" He, agape,
Over his shoulder bawled, "To Golgotha!"

v

On a hilltop there stood three crosses, ranked
Against a ponderous thundercloud that rolled
Its folds across the north. The crowd, content,
Hurled insults at the midmost, whereon hung
The Preacher. There a man from time to time
Lifted a sponge dripping in vinegar
And held it to His lips. Soldiers with shining helms
Ranked on the hilltop, kept their swords unsheathed,
Fearing the mob might rush the crosses, work
New vengeance on the sufferer. Lazarus

Drew closer, fascinated. In his heart
Still burned the unasked question: "Why was I
Summoned from death's peace back to tedious life
And given no reason?" but now pity swept
The question from his lips at sight of that
Forlorn face, buffeted, defiled, and torn,
Staring with fixed glance at the blackening sky.
Whereon pale lightnings danced. Long moments
    ebbed,
Then from that throat there burst a doleful cry,
"My God, my God, why hast Thou forsaken me?"
The crowd roared back its laughter for an answer.
But Lazarus started, spurning them aside,
Sped to where stood the soldiery; there turned
And shouted loud: "Hear me, you fools; I lay
Fast in the grave, stone-dead for four long days,
And this Man who had eaten at my house,
Because He loved me, came and to life gave back
My body. Wherefore is this done to Him?
He hangs here innocent of aught but good,
A mighty prophet. I here pledge my life
Freely for His." A hurtling shower of stones
At these words came from out the surging mob.
One hit him on the breast. Dizzy and sick he fell,
Thinking, "This now is death." A red-faced soldier
    near
Struck at the body, kicked it to a ditch
Filled with dry thorn. It rolled within and sank.
At which the delighted mob howled their applause.

VI

Long he lay there, quite senseless. When he woke,
It was dark night, the sky was full of stars;
Empty and bare and solemn stood the hill,
The crosses gone, the mob had wandered home.
Tomorrow was the feast. His hands and feet
Were torn with thorns. The stone had cut a gash
Under his right breast, bruised was his forehead and
Each move he made was pain. He slowly dragged
His body out, and painfully strove to stand,
Not knowing what to do. Jerusalem's gates were
     closed.
Till suddenly he saw before him, standing near,
Two officers with a squad. He crouched again
Behind a balk of rock and heard their words:—
"Some of these crazy Jews still seem to think
This Man was the Messiah; though yet more
Deny Him, still the mob begins to waver,
Just when their work is done. I always said
That madman Lazarus should have been put to
     death,
Before he had a chance to speak, for now
His words begin to unsettle their wits again;
This brainsick people will think anything
That tends to our discredit. Pontius
Has cause now to regret that he insisted
On that inscription. Besides, his wife's been at him,
Swearing he acted rashly. I have never seen
A man so shaken. He now fears these Jews

May steal the body, show it to the mob,
And cause fresh riots: and I quite agree
They might do anything. So our course is clear:
To find that tomb of Joseph and to take
The body up, and throw it down an old dry well
Far hence and cast great stones upon it. Joseph's
    tomb,
A new-cut one, lies hereabouts, they say."

VII

He saw the body taken from the tomb,
He heard the stone roll back, caught in the light
Of glimmering torches, a gleam of the pale face
Unrolled from the linen grave-clothes. The lieu-
    tenant
Who spoke before gave orders, and the men
Chuckled admiringly at the Governor's guile,
Swearing, "By Hercules, we'll fool these Jews!"
The clothes were dropped upon the threshold and
The door was left rolled back. Dull footfalls faded
Far down the valley. What could he do or say?
He was too weak to stand. One only thought
Beat in his brain, to crawl somewhere and sleep.
The tomb left open was more safe than here,
For stray wolves on the roads had torn the flesh
Of drowsy travellers recently. So now,
With spent force, groaning, every inch a pang,
He dragged himself, and dropping on the stone,
Sank in an instant into dreamless sleep.

VIII

Dawn kindled in the east as he awoke;
The Sabbath had gone by while still he lay
Exhausted, filled with the long dreamless rest
That knits together worn-out flesh and soul;
Now once again he woke and heard the birds
Twittering among the thorn trees. He was hungry,
But the grey dew of the morning cooled his lips,
On his torn feet he found that he could stand.
It seemed to him a low voice sounded in
His head that said, "Go forward, Lazarus,
Still is there much to do, much to endure;
Life's game is good, though there be no reward."
He staggered to the doorway of the tomb
And paused. Before him stood a woman. Tears
    ran down
Her face, and in dark mourning she was clad.
He muttered, "What is this? What do you want?"
Whereat she answered:—"Sir, if you know where
My Master has been borne, show me the place."
And then she looked at him and suddenly saw
Gashes in hands and feet, within his side
A red rent, and dark scratches on his brows;
She gasped at him "Rabboni," fell to earth.
Dazed and distracted, he cried, "Touch me not."

IX

That evening, when the light was faint and spent,
Two of the disciples, weary, sick at heart,

John Gould Fletcher

Trudged homeward from Jerusalem to the inn
At Emmaus—and as they went they saw
A figure going before them, bowed upon
A heavy staff. In the close gathering dusk
They hailed him as a stranger. He drew near,
And saw their faces wet with tears, their foreheads
    darkened
With lines of pain and care. He asked them why
They seemed so grieved, and they began explaining
Of Jesus' deeds, and how He had been done to death,
And how that very morning Mary had come
To Joseph's tomb, and seen Him risen again,
And the tomb empty, and how others after
Had looked into the tomb but found Him not.
Now Lazarus' heart pained in him, but to speak
The truth and perish. But some outer force
Greater than night or armies, held his tongue.
So the disciples drew near to the inn,
Where they abode, and seeing their guest halted
Upon his feet, bade him come in and share
A room with them. The roads were full of wolves
And robbers. Lazarus wearily agreed.
And here they sat at meat and Lazarus stretched
Both his torn hands to grasp the bread which he
Half-famished longed for; but the disciples saw
Prints as of jagged nails and stared into his face.
Thorn-marks were on his brow; his lips were pale.
They stammered "Master!" but no answer came,
The stranger had uprisen hastily
And without word had rushed forth to the night.

X

This was the house where Mary had said there came
The disciples for their meetings. Simon's house.
And from behind this door, there softly rose
The sound of prayers and singing. Long he stood
Before the shut door, then he slowly knocked,
And said: "Peace unto all within." The door was
    opened
A narrow crack, and, in the timorous hush,
He stalked into the room. Full on him beat the
    light
Of lamps and torches. Before fifty pairs of eyes
He stood. His robes were rent, in his right side
A red gash showed. Upon his brow was blood,
And in his hands and feet were deep thorn-piercings
Unhealed. He spread out wide his arms,
And looking on them cried out: "Who am I?
Speak if you know my name!" A great hush fell;
But suddenly a haggard, hawk-faced man
Rushed forward with a cry, pressed his cold fingers
Into the red wound, felt the thorn-torn hands,
And sobbing stammered out: "My Master and my
    God."

XI

And after that, no more did Lazarus say
Of that which he had been: he bore his cross
Of silence, watching still the glad bright faces
82

Of those who held him Jesus risen in truth
From out the tomb.   He smiled and kept his peace;
He blessed them weeping inwardly, smiled, was dumb
For ever. . . .

John Gould Fletcher

TO A SURVIVOR OF THE FLOOD

SET high your head above the nameless flood,
And brood upon its empty waters; lean
Your forehead back and stare aloof, serene,
At night's betrayal; now let the stagnant blood
Beat in your smouldering heart which sunken far
Beneath the surface, hammers weak and cold
Against your buried ribs, long washed and rolled
By waters of Wormwood, that old fallen star.

Night brings no rainbows—you within the night,
Last Titan standing on wrecked peaks upright,
Olympus piled on Sinai, can you find
Aught but the moonless dark to match your mind?
Who knows, who knows?   When all the gods have
     gone,
And man's despair has riven apart the sun,
And you, vain atom, are grown Everyman,
Is this the beginning or the end you scan?
Will you speed forth on some chance lava flow
Torn from a ruined sun you do not know,
Towards a state no human tongue can tell
After wrecked heaven has fallen below dead hell?
Or will you sink down sluggishly within,
Dropping below the waters cheek and chin,
And last of all, now nevermore to rise,
The huge unspeaking orbits of your eyes?
Will you rest rotting darkly in that sea,
To an eternity of vacancy?

84

John Gould Fletcher

PAINTED WOMEN

THESE are our sisters of sin and charity,
With reddened lips and painted cheeks they go
Dressed in such poor cheap finery
As mocks the sodden hopes that sleep below;
Their deeds of grace God's eyes will surely mark,
Although none has a place to lay her head
Unless it be within lust's bitter dark
And loathly bed.

These are our sisters of sin and charity,
With mincing steps they march along the street
Proclaiming themselves shameless whores. But we,
From the dark horror out of which they greet
Each daybreak, make anew
A living song of praise to some dead Christ
To whom be thanks we are not as these who
Are nightlong sacrificed.

These are our sisters. Hurl your taunt of scorn,
But look upon the dust beneath that bears,
Out of corruption, shining ears of corn
And takes your bodies as it takes your prayers.
You may win heaven. These have doubtless hell.
Yet even the devils might wipe off those tears that
    swell
Into the eyes of these abandoned ones
Before they ease the chastity of your sons.

85

John Gould Fletcher

BEFORE OLYMPUS

Across the sky run streaks of white light, aching;
Across the earth the chattering grass is sprawling;
Across the sea roll troubled gleams awaking,
Across the steeps dark broken shapes are crawling.

We have been scourged with youth, a rod in pickle
To cut the hide from our own hearts. We know
The tree of life is also cursed. We heed
The silent laughter of grey gods of time.

We do not seek the lithe and brittle music
Of swords and flame. We have no more desire
For glory or contempt. The moment flies
Past us, and shouting carries its echo on.

The clank of wheels and pumps, the screech of
    levers
No longer now afflicts our inmost bearing;
The old wise nightingales have longer ears,
They sing the blooming of wild immortelles.

And through the desolation of great cities
As in a madhouse we go peering where
Black butterflies flit about a carcass. Words
Gallop about the sky. The earth broods like a
    stone.

John Gould Fletcher

Heaven is a blank news-sheet fixed and trembling
Between the knees of God.   The grass runs crawling.
The waves of the sea their laughter are dissembling,
But who will reap them when our scythes are fall-
    ing?

ALFRED KREYMBORG

Alfred Kreymborg

PARALLELS

SOME day I'll have to stop you on the street
Or you will simply pass me when we meet;

But meanwhile I have still just grace enough
To fill a faded room like this with stuff

To bring you back and hold you where the toy
I am in being fondled kindles joy,

As some small pastime might in a mere boy
Whose love of flame no candle can destroy.

Another woman has another way
Of giving man the thing I needn't say;

Most any woman knows the roundelay
For buying what she has to buy and pay

The man who has his lustrous night entire
At so much for the bargain and the fire.

But I'm in a caprice to give you more
Than even I have given you before:

To prove or not to prove that I can move
A man who comes for me to come for love,

Or show, perhaps, if only for the whim,
That she who offers this might care for him

And come to him no longer in the guise
One tightens round the self until it dies.

My candour tends to spoil your holiday?
And yet it's not for talk I'd have you stay.

Let me pour you a second cup of tea
And improvise a better thought of me.

I'd mould my fancy an accustomed vein;
But shouldn't I be sure to entertain

A visitor like you with variation?
Avoid a bit repeating a relation?

Isn't it thus the arts refine in Asia?
Sagacity resourceful as a geisha?

Not even priests eschew insinuation
Of some quite novel method of libation.

I digress? Where was I? What did I say?
You really don't mind having me this way?

It soothes you? Does it truly? I'd have meant
To play our commonplace an instrument

Alfred Kreymborg

As subtle as a clavichord or spinet,
With many spider-grained illusions in it

Reflecting haunting webs of shadowed fire
For slowly rousing delicate desire.

Why shouldn't one wear silk between the skin
And that possession man would enter in?

And mustn't one be careful not to wean
His thought from the fictitious go-between,

The puzzle for the mind to circumvent,
Lest ardour, gaining all at once, be spent?

You smile a little, corners of you flicker.
How sensitive you are and so much quicker.

Consoling after all it is to give
Oneself to one who lets a hope or grief

Indulge in melancholy mockery,
Then break its brittle walls like crockery.

Now rest your head a while among the pillows
And I'll cease imitating moaning willows.

I merely thought when you came in the door,
When you came in just as you've done before,

That somehow one man might learn to revere
A lover who could save love falling sere,

A man who'd go so far as to adore
The woman who would not degrade a chore;

For isn't she, when love is that, a wife,
Or one who gropes along the street for life?

There's nothing in this mood to bring you sorrow
Or cause you to regret to-night to-morrow.

Let me draw that dark shade across your eyes
And keep them and the sun from growing wise.

The sun at twilight is a yellow ring,
And pessimism is a mellow thing.

I'd have instead a candle in the room;
A slender moon-like handle for the gloom

To flutter, widen, soften to a curtain,
To hide what may transpire and still be certain

That what we do is neither you nor I,
And what we don't do isn't all a lie.

It needs but such a sly white artifice
To mark that we have reached an old abyss

In which there's naught of romance to endanger
A careless move or turn each stranger stranger.

The hushed event will yield to you and me
No more than what we were, each body free.

And I am here beside you praying only
That I won't seem too far and you too lonely.

What have I said to make you sigh and stare?
You'd better stretch full-length and unaware,

And feel the blood start tingling in your toes,
And feel it mount and go to where love goes.

As for myself, I love them thus; my feet
Seem far away; the length of some long street.

And doesn't life itself begin like this?
And death as well come on with such a kiss?

All verticals lie down in front of him
Whenever his head nears and has the whim?

I'm only improvising—see—I laugh—
And what I've said, consider it as chaff.

You want me to be quiet now? Of course.
And silence is at last the best divorce.

Alfred Kreymborg

SEVEN MOVEMENTS

Neighbors

BIRDS aren't people one has to walk to:
Stay where you are, they'll come to you, talk too.

What's in gadding in search of a neighbor?
Far too much distance, much too much labor.

Chat about trifles, argue a season:
Surely you'll find no roots to grow trees on?

All conclusions descend to the trivial,
Unless they sing and the song's convivial.

So don't stray off, but sit down and be swayed
By idleness eyeing a fiery parade

Of robins, swallows, thrushes, sparrows,
Coming like lightning, going like arrows.

Alfred Kreymborg

Hermit Thrush

It's hard to count what an air can do:
It cannot buy one a shirt or shoe:

It cannot bind a neat nest; find things
For leaving the earth on floating wings:

Nothing of twigs in it, nothing of roots;
But something of rivers, a little of flutes,

That I've heard rippling a bodiless tune,
That gathered me into a small balloon,

And took me high without writing a check,
Then let me down without breaking my neck:

No effort at all: I was absent-minded:
Don't even know now what the air or the wind did.

Alfred Kreymborg

Peewee

Is it a wish—that tiny tin whistle
Out on a leafless branch throwing a missile,

Wrapped in a dip and a lift, like a bow
Of rain turned somersault, curve down below:

Tip-dip-tipping a phrase and a blow,
Releasing a flute in a piccolo,

And striking an ear with a short, thin dart,
Pinning a secret one hides in a heart?

If it isn't a wish, why does it tarry?
If it wasn't fulfilled, how far did it carry?

Was it too stunted to be sentimental?
Or much too local to be continental?

Alfred Kreymborg

Robin

HE takes a lot of staccato steps, stops—
Like a busy toe-dancer with dizzy tops,

That never cease spinning, twinkling a minute,
Until they come to the end of what's in it.

He runs on a line like a tight-rope walker;
Tries not to look scared; nor to answer a talker.

He might be as deaf as a man who surveys
Two spots with a string for the high wire ways.

No matter how fast he may go or stop dead—
He holds his head still—an oblivious head;

But just down below, they twist and they squirm—
Like a terrified crowd—or an angleworm.

Alfred Kreymborg

City Chap

Who's that dusty stranger?   What's he doing here?
That city-bred bird with the ill-bred leer?

Perching on branches like telegraph wires?
Chirping his slang above passionate fires?

Poking his head about, twitching his tail,
Getting drunk in our pools as if they were ale?

Never accepting, but stealing our rations?
Acting toward us as he would to relations?

Who asked him hither, what led him this way?
With his critical carping, his mockery, eh?

And worse than all these, he's a jerky reminder
Of winters, towns, and of people no kinder.

Alfred Kreymborg

Swallows

THEY'RE not going travelling for many a day:
They don't attempt branches, they seek it in clay:

First they start holes and then dig in hollows:
Excavate caverns to lay future swallows:

A gray, crumbling chapel, best for the landing:
Too old for man—not too old to be standing:

A haunt no one visits, come west or come east,
Unless he be harmless, some hermit or priest

Who walks in a plot shaded green, an area
Between pater noster and ave maria.

If he should look up and see birds, the chance is,
He'll be but a lover: another St. Francis.

Alfred Kreymborg

Song Sparrow

HE stutters and stammers—a catch in his throat—
Chromatics falter—too many notes float—

Beginnings too eager—scales all uncertain—
Come to a cadence, too careful the curtain.

The thing that he studies—flattering, fluttering—
Might be called song could the fellow but sing

From the start of a phrase to the end of a sentence,
And not be pursued and caught up by repentance.

Who would consider such doings professional?
The little he does, does it sound processional?

And still.he persists and resists till he find
A channel for opening the way to his mind.

VACHEL LINDSAY

Vachel Lindsay

THE FLOWER-FED BUFFALOES

THE flower-fed buffaloes of the spring
In the days of long ago,
Ranged where the locomotives sing
And the prairie flowers lie low;
The tossing, blooming, perfumed grass
Is swept away by wheat,
Wheels and wheels and wheels spin by
In the spring that still is sweet.
But the flower-fed buffaloes of the spring
Left us long ago.
They gore no more, they bellow no more,
They trundle around the hills no more:—
With the Blackfeet lying low,
With the Pawnees lying low.

THESE ARE THE YOUNG

(Dedicated to the Reverend Charles Pease, Minister of the
Unitarian Society, Spokane, Washington.)

I

"WHAT new mob disturbs the days?
Who are these, with intrusive ways,
Who speak with an alien tongue?
Who are these Olympian-white
Butterflies of flame,
High upon Sun Mountain,
Invading now, every fountain,
Obeying their own captains
And to no man tame;
Whispering so low
We cannot hear at all,
Yet calling 'Brother,' 'Sister'
Through the sun-mountain wall?
Who are these Olympian-white
Butterflies of flame,
Full of a holy grace?
Tell me their spiritual name."

*"This is a separate race,
Speaking an alien tongue
These are the young!"*

As you will find those mirrors in each home
Wherever in dim heaven you may roam.

In heaven will meet that imp you meet each day,
That strange, inquiring face, eager to play,

The *You*, you struggle with, you love and hate
And wonder at her traits, and dodge her fate.

III

So get acquainted now.   Take endless hours
Loving your wonders, like a spray of flowers.

Take two long mirrors, study your soul's air,
Be not content just fixing your back hair.

So, young America, say: "I am I,
Columbia through a thousand years of sky.

"When I'm grown up, still I will fix my hair
With two long mirrors on the crystal stair.

"I will have six wings to match my grace,
Blue-tipped to match the eyes of my soul's face."

IV

But this is outside.   Deeper far will be
Shadows and whimsies you will learn to see

And judge by every throb and hidden line
If you are growing wiser, more divine.

V

So let us find sweet glory in each glass,
Living with wonders, let no noonday pass

Without a seeking with more love and deeper
To find our dreams, on to the inmost sleeper.

VI

There are a hundred Americas to-day
And each one may lead up the heavenly way.

We may find them in most common reels,—
Heroes with velvet heels or iron heels!

We may find them as the reels roll by
And comedies will bear our wings on high,

Dreams look out from films as from a glass
Thousands of dreams!   A thousand years may
    pass!

Dreams that will teach us writing, painting,
    song,
And plans for building lovingly and long.

Vachel Lindsay

VII

Our future is no book-made future. No,
All books are but the record and the flow

Of thoughts that flash from the Egyptian eye,
The tall soul, when it holds your mirrors high.

VIII

I know there are great mirrors in the sky
We will be writing by.

Americans in the seventh sky put on
Six extra wings and a long cloak of dawn.

IX

Now let us make her glass, now spread in view
The films that will her wonders still renew,

The films where we will see each hour return-
ing
Her beauties with sweet vanity all burning.

X

Flags are the ancient symbols of our pride,
But this long film is greater far beside.

This, the new art, shall show the new-born soul,
America, with her special aureole,

With wings, new wings, now lifting toward the sky,
America, the Psyche-butterfly,
America, the Psyche-butterfly.

Vachel Lindsay

AMERICA DRESSES FOR THE BALL

I

Oh, dewy fern and Violet's Breath,
Conqueror of stupid death,
I think how your mirror, Violet's Breath,—
Misty with the twilight's veil,—
Shows your beauty, ivory pale,—
Your fairy profile lifted high,
Whimsical Psyche-butterfly.
It shows your beauty, white and red,
Your bobbing head, your bended head,
Your eyes so wide in the dove-light
Soft, yet made for proud delight,
Your mouth the size of a fairy's dime,
Your fingers rippling like a rime;
Setting your evening dress in place,
Your swaying grace, your preening grace,
Fixing your feathers, like a swan,
Fixing your silver slippers on.

II

Go out and have one lovely time,
Your whole life rippling like a rime;
Whatever ball they take you to,
There, among the humors new,
I send my soul to dance with you.
None are so close, none have such fire

They can outwit me in desire,
Or will get past me in the soft
And holy lights, always aloft,
There to crown your pretty head,
Your bobbing head, your bended head.
Like me or love me, as you will,
I will be dancing with you still,
Glittering there, the first, the last;
None will get past me, none get past,
Because I come on wings of air,
Never there, always there.

III

But, lady dancing on the cloud,
You must be always high and proud,
And so my endless name for you,
Must still be Young America,
This is the name I call you there ·
When I come on wings of air,
Never there, always there.

IV

Oh, when at two you reach your house
And stand as still as a white mouse
Before your mirror once again,
Gone are the dancing village men;
But stare into your mirror, stare,
My shadow waits before you there,
Never there, always there.

Vachel Lindsay

IN MEMORY OF A GOOD PRINTER

(N. M. Naylor of Springfield, Illinois. Died December 3, 1924.)

BROTHER, we take our earthly farewell now,
Brother, buried in a Springfield grave,
And always buried in your craftsman's vow,
By choice, and not necessity, a slave.

Never could I have been a man like that.
I always liked to strut, and blow my horn,
And make my lion out of every cat,
And call each horse my personal unicorn.

Yours was the broken heart, the faithful hand,
Colossal patience, and the printer's pride.
Your inks were always black, your papers grand,
Your margins always straight and proud and wide.

You knew a thousand ways to go to press,
And every one was novel, clean and fine.
You could untangle fat fools in a mess,
Could make their silly copy stand in line.

You made the bleared zinc etchings come out
    right,
Made honest half-tones out of tin-type smears.
While rich men cursed you, you could be polite,
In short, a printer, through the years and years.

Vachel Lindsay

I always dreamed my books like strange pine-
        brands,
American buffaloes, fairies, Buffalo Bill.
I always hoped that your fraternal hands,
Following the copy up and down the hill,

Would pile my fires and keep my dragons high,
Produce my hieroglyphics the right way.
Who now will make Old Springfield's pamphlets fly?
The notice of your funeral comes today.

Men like to think, with a good old-fashioned sigh
Of homely customs in the better land.
And so, old-fashionedly, we prophesy
Of your stern, patient, and correcting hand.

You give Mark Twain's long cuss-words ample space,
No editing angels hold you, or refine,
And print proud Altgeld's word without disgrace,
And make as brilliant Wilson's sternest line.

They scrawl cartoons, debate, and write in flame
Then rush to press. You, gently, print them right.
Even in Heaven you do not sign your name.
Dear N. M. Naylor, this is my good-night:—

There you will have one friend—the Crucified.
Your quiet toil the Christ will understand.
Yours is the loving heart, the wounded side,
Yours is the broken heart, the faithful hand.
118

Vachel Lindsay

THE VOYAGE

WHAT is my mast?   A pen.
What are my sails?   Ten crescent moons.
What is my sea?   A bottle of ink.
Where do I go?   To heaven again.
What do I eat?   The amaranth flower.
While the winds through the jungles think old tunes
I eat that flower with ivory spoons.
While the winds through the jungles play old tunes;
The songs the angels used to sing
When heaven was not old autumn, but spring—
The bold, old songs of heaven and spring.

AMY LOWELL

Born February 9, 1874
Died May 12, 1925

Amy Lowell

A COMMUNICATION

You deceived me handsomely
With your inconsolable grief at parting.
I really believed in your crocodile tears
And suffered at the exhibition of your suffering;
A little for myself also at the breaking of an old tie,
A habit grown as comfortably pleasant
As the wearing of a friendly dressing-gown.
For we had passed the stage of exhilaration
And reached the solace of a quiet domesticity.
I was prepared to linger over it in retrospect,
Not too unhappily, for had we not agreed a thousand
      times
That this sundering was merely geographical.
And now a month has passed and not a word have I
      had from you,
Not so much as a scrawl to say you could not write!

Fate lays innumerable springes for persons of imagi-
      nation.
Because I wished to believe,
I saw in your Byronic gesture of woe,
Not what it purported to be, certainly,
But something not too different.
You cast a larger shadow than yourself, that I
      realized,
But even I, who should have known better,
Believed it was your shadow.

I crave your pardon for my blunder.
The mask was well assumed,
I should have been critical enough to understand it
    was an artistic production.
I congratulate you on the verisimilitude of it,
But I shall not be fooled again, be sure of that.
In future I shall see you as you are:
A plaster figure of a man that's grown a little dusty.
We all have knick-knacks round which once meant
    something.
It is rather a wrench to take them from their niches,
But life goes on, imperious, and bric-à-brac accumu-
    lates.
Still, because I cherished you once, I will not throw
    you away just yet.
I will put you on an upper shelf in the pantry of
    my mind,
Among old flower-vases I no longer use, being of a
    bygone fashion.
It may interest you to know that the place you
    occupied
Looks a little strange to me without you,
But that, of course, will pass.

Amy Lowell

THE SIBYL

SHE was an aggressively unattractive old woman,
Sitting there behind the table in the hotel corridor.
Nothing could make her interesting or pathetic,
Although to be on duty at midnight
Proved her lot unfortunate.
From her topknot of grey, escaping, withered hair
To her fat, delaying hands,
She precluded pathos;
Even her melancholy attempt at finery,
A faded imitation coral necklace,
Seemed only dirty and dull.
Hers was a hard lot indeed,
Yet I could not pity her.
I asked for a pencil.
She gave me one, and grudged the doing it heartily.
When I reached my room, I found that the pencil
    had a rubber on the end.
Cursed old sibyl!
What do you mean by uttering prophecies
At midnight,
In a hotel corridor!

PASTIME

> *"Whose pretty pawn is this,*
> *And what shall be done to redeem it?"*
> Children's Game.

I AM immoderately fond of this place.
My thoughts run under it like the roots of trees and
    grasses,
They spread above it like fluttering, inconsequential
    leaves.
Spring comes to me with the blossoming of the
    snowdrop under the arbor-vitæ.
So all Springs come, and ever must do.
Spring ripens with the crocus cups on the South
    lawn,
Blue and white crocuses, remains of an ancient
    garden,
By the side of an ancient house—
So they told me, so I believed.
That shadowy structure holds a distant charm,
I see its walls printed upon the air, in certain moods,
And build it back into solidity with awed enjoy-
    ment.
But that is fairy-tale or history,
And I am more concerned with recollection.

How perpetually the seasons mark themselves!
Tulips for April,
Peonies for May.

The pillar-rose has not lacked its robin's-nest since
    I remember,
Nor the pink horse-chestnut its mob of honey-bees:
The boom of them is essence of sleep and flowers,
Of Summer sleep and poetry mixed together.
Yet there are differences even in the repeated lilt
    of time.
I seem to think the humming-birds are fewer,
And I have not seen a luna-moth for years.

Now, suddenly, here is a grosbeak
Perched in the double-cherry near the door.
He suggests that I look him over,
His striped black and white,
His rose-red triangle of waistcoat.
He is clearly on view for commendation,
Displaying himself as though I were his wife or his
    tailor
Observing to pronounce a verdict.
I had contemplated second childhood,
But scarcely believed it imminent,
And here I am plunged in it.
A rose-breasted grosbeak indeed,
And the last I saw was in that long, first childhood.
Senility may have its compensations,
I shall hunt up my old butterfly-net
And prowl about to-night seeking luna-moths.

Amy Lowell

APOTHEOSIS

THE mountains were both far and high,
Their jagged peaks along the sky
Broke it like splintered porphyry.

I stood beneath a cherry tree
Whose thick leaves fluttered ceaselessly,
And there were cherry clusters—three.

Prone at my feet was one who slept;
At my right hand, a maid who wept;
And at my left, a youth who kept

Vigil before a naked sword
Which gleamed and sparkled on the sward
As though it were a holy word.

An eery moonlight lit the place,
Just bright enough to show each face
And each lithe body's proper grace.

The weeping maiden raised her head:
"I die for want of food," she said,
And in her famished gaze I read

The wasting of her life in tears.
Her face was shattered as though years
Had nicked it with an iron shears.

Amy Lowell

"Peace, Mournful Lady," I replied,
"Within these leaves dark cherries hide."
I raised my hand, but in a stride,

Catching his sword up, so he came,
The youth. His helmet burst to flame,
And on it shone a fearful name.

The maiden moaned and sank beneath
The tree's foot, like a fallen wreath
Of myrtle-buds, stripped of their sheath.

Once more we were as we had been:
One wept, one slept, one watched his keen
Sword lying in the grasses green.

Then she who slumbered stirred and woke,
And throwing back her ample cloak
She lifted heavy eyes and spoke:

"I faint for hunger," whispered she,
"And though above me I can see
Cherries, I am spent utterly.

Reach me the fruit for kindness, so
My blood may once more course and flow
As it was used, oh, long ago."

The words were faint as is the jar
Of air behind a falling star
Felt in a forest where ghosts are.

"Be still," I answered, "if I fail
To succour you, no burning mail
Will be the force to which I quail."

Brave words to whip my spirit on.
Under the leaves the cherries shone.
A moment and I should have done.

But, as the thought came, so did he,
And stood beside the cherry tree,
And struck his sword upon her knee.

Even while she fell, he went his way,
And laid his sword as erst it lay,
And mournfully awaited day.

Then, drearily, above the rim
Of mountains, rose a sun so dim
I only knew day watching him.

For, as the morning slowly grew,
He took another ghastly hue,
And what was pale had turned to blue.

His corselet was corroded rust,
Between his greaves a briar thrust
Its long head up, his eyes were dust.

His sword still lay upon the ground,
But all at once it moved and wound
Among the grass-blades to a mound

Dead and gone and should be let lie,
Not swinging and smirking after other men's scrib-
    blings.
Sailor blue and star,
To tell the world here's an inn to stop at,
And a young fellow blazing his eyes blind in a worm-
    hole
After something he can't see.
Pretty world he's made for me to swing in,
Smirking at him with my star that's only paint
When the bells toll of a Sunday,
And a grinning church-yard underneath
Rots the man I was.
Can he cheat it when his time's come,
Or will he, too, be strung up on a pair of whining
    hinges,
Sailor blue and star, or something like it?
Ding-dong bell on a sign-board,
And the old goose gobbled full of papers
Waddling down to the ditch.
That's a song for a Sunday morning,
Come swing, come smirk, till your boards give way,
And you go to grind shoe-leather,
And the wind can't peck you from the dust.
Grand world, come swing, come smirk,
Baby Bunting world of painted nonsense,
Up and down to a scrape of rusty bearings
Like a man with a cold at the back of his nose;
Holy-ghost world with a star on it like a cold pan-
    cake,

And the devil's beer brewed of sick brains
Which should be let lie and aren't,
And go for the choking of geese
Laid out stark in a green ditch
Of a Sunday morning for the church-folk to see.

EDNA ST. VINCENT MILLAY

JOHN CROWE RANSOM

TWO GENTLEMEN IN BONDS

Pink and Pale

PAUL, pinked with dozing, stood from the chair
    wherein
Digestion was assisted after lunch—
Roast chine and gravies, pudding, swigs of punch,
His manhood being strong and it no sin
To feed—Paul stretched and tucked his loose ends in
And singing till he had sung himself outside
He went to banter Abbott, or to ride;
Poor company Abbott kept his nearest of kin.

For everything that Paul was, Abbott was not.
His legs were two long straws, his face was chalk,
He would not ride, nor run, nor drowse, but walk
The field in thought more passionate than another's;
You hadn't believed that two such men were broth-
    ers;
Yet it was credited, the same sire begot.

John Crowe Ransom

Thinking, Drinking

A young girl cousined them, whose character was
A wise bright head and grey eyes beautifuller
To Paul than his brave manhood seemed to her,
Though he was Greek enough for Phidias,
And she could ride; but about this Michaelmas
She wouldn't run quick and green in riding habit
To canter with him, and hollo to every rabbit
That bounced across to thicket or to grass.

She listened too much to Abbott's music of words,
Savage and strange. "How noble is man thinking!
But we, my cousin, are filled with eating and drink-
    ing.
Should we not read philosophy?" But Paul said,
"Edith, my brother's a fool, and out of his head,"
And saw her thoughts fly over him, like the birds.

John Crowe Ransom

In Air

But Abbott when he sought him was nowhere.
Paul said not all his eggs therefore were addled,
Not much: "For let my gelding Trey be saddled."
And he flies like a young rich landlord god on air,
The earth his wealth, ethereal, yet aware
Of the tread of the dark wood mold and turfy rye,
Rich smell of horse in his nostril, wind in his eye,
And galloping through the autumn all his care.

The country beauty flushed him up to the ears.
He put the gelding to the hurdles, and Trey
Must take them every one in Paul's own way,
For if his spirit failed him and he shrank,
Right back Paul drove him rowelling his flank;
But clicking the boards he gave his master fears.

John Crowe Ransom

Thought, Distraught

Abbott proceeded soberly, with rhyme.
He heard the lone birds' cries, and his own tongue
Made melancholy more than the birds had sung.
The man could talk in Latin, music, mime,
Or sonneteer with Petrarch in his prime,
He had a prince's powers, but what he willed
Was to go down to dust with the unfulfilled
Rather than stint himself with space and time.

He was a specter gibbering under trees
Which preened their yellow foliage, while he
    thought,
"Flutter then, flutter, for you shall fly distraught."
He waved his black sleeves like an evil prophet,
Death in his every verse or not far off it;
Quite down he hung his own head, mortal as these.

John Crowe Ransom

Meeting in a Garden

"Garden of no fruit!   Lichen on a stone!
And what is life but a barren laborious tree
Too streaked and scored with black mortality?"
Abbott said several dooms with firm intone,
And had more worlds to sentence, he had not done,
When *trot, trot, trot,* and squeezing under the wicket
Where one peach hung there came a fellow to pick it;
It was his heathen brother, famished and blown.

Paul had a smile always in waiting.   "Brother,
Can you have kept this only peach for me?
If you want half of it though, I will agree."
But Abbott wanted nothing, he never took pleasure,
And now he glared on Paul and took his measure;
There was a fool in the family, one or the other.

John Crowe Ransom

Epithalamion of a Peach

She was small, ripe, round, a maid not maculate
Saving her bright cheeks, but the rude bridegroom
Claims her, his heavy hand has led her home.
Nor did he pull her gently through his gate
As had a lover dainty and delicate:
The two-and-thirty cut-throats doing his will
Tore off her robe and stripped her bare until
Drunken with appetite, he devoured and ate.

A pleasant slaver drools from off his tongue
Where he has eaten the admirable peach
That nested high, but could not foil his reach;
His sharp work was unloverly, bringing the wry
To squeamish Abbott's face; unnoticed by
The oblivious gelding stamping in his dung.

John Crowe Ransom

Swine, Wine

In that country it happening that the King
Came now that way victorious from battle,
Where he had slain some folk and stolen their cattle,
His chamberlain told Sir Paul an excellent thing
To do: Make ready with feast and furnishing
To lodge the King three days, and it was good
If the King favored his bed and relished his food,
For service helps a man in the sight of the King.

Now purple and linen, heifers, poultry, swine,
Paul loved not for themselves, but he loved yet,
As he hated his belly empty and his skin wet;
It would impoverish his great country house
If the State descended for a week's carouse;
No more he napped in innocence after wine.

John Crowe Ransom

L'état C'est Moi

Abbott previsioning the pestiferous swarm
Of royal locusts: "Expect now, Brother Paul,
A trifling inconvenience, that is all.
These levies and taxes keep you out of harm;
The thieves the King has slain cannot alarm
His people now; but you pay for this relief;
Strong governments must always eat much beef;
On n'a de beaux états qu'avec gendarmes.

"It doesn't matter that your King's a fraud,
A great pig's-bladder prickable as any,
A man whose nose runs probably more than many,
Whose beard is soused with gravy. He is the King,
He is the State, you are his littlest thing,
His man, else excommunicate and outlawed."

John Crowe Ransom

Misanthropy

"But I am no King's-man, Paul; I am amazed
We sovereignties should let them rule and range.
In the mother-house I dwelt severe and strange,
With cries was torn from my quiet cavern, ill-
    pleased;
A Form whose fixity everywhere is teased
With change—am enamored yet of that dark
    womb—
Devise no analogue but one—the tomb,
Where Kings are put to sleep and kingdoms razed.

"My compliments to your King. Say I'm not in.
I'll to your topmost Northern tower, a misanthrope
Too firm to wheedle a fat King or lean Pope,
And all the Pope's prayers and all the King's power
Shall not seduce me out of my grim grey tower;
But you have delicate skin, so save your skin."

John Crowe Ransom

Vain Protestations

"What sort of notion is this, Abbott, dear man?
It isn't as if one had to bring oneself
To kiss the royal bottom of the Guelph,
Can't you control your devils any better than
To sputter this obscene blab, you Caliban,
And hadn't you rather acknowledge a higher power
By simple gesture than mould in your ratty tower
In cold and loneliness and hate unchristian?"

"But no, Cousin Paul! You can't scare a man like
    him,
That isn't the way. Abbott, for your brother's sake,
For the tenants, the land, a father's good name, don't
    make
A breach in the etiquette of the royal visit—
But, Paul! there's something splendid about this—
    or is it
Terrible, rather—or eerie—or what synonym?"

John Crowe Ransom

Fait Accompli

He sent for Edith—it was Paul's desire—
And found her very young, coming with face flushed
And her grey films averted and the storm hushed
In which she had cried like Abbott by the fire
To a maid smoothing her tangles and attire
How these incredible Kings destroyed your peace,
They bent the body and soul; death would release,—
Now the King sees the wild one caught in his wire.

He's taken Edith's little hand, to lay
In Paul's capacious. Hope now for no recourse,
My girl! Paul the Possessor. For better for worse.
Does the strange girl smile? "I wish you many
        joys;
My kingdom shall be greater by many boys
If Heaven reward this union as I pray."

John Crowe Ransom

Implacable Tower

What from the tower? "Fool, Fool, I say to the man
That mightily scares his dog and horse and churl
But stumbles mortally on one big-eyed girl,
A flowing vine, uncaptured though well he can
Inscribe her ghost-white buds in his hand-span,
Killing him with cool innocence and able to deject
The vainglorious captain that had stood stiff-necked
Even to a King at court; Fool, Fool, to the man."

Paul took his wine and slept, and his thought
    swirled
From dream to dream through Christendom. But
    Paul's bride
Climbed up, with a great rat scampering at her side,
Reached the top step of Abbott's Northern tower
And listening at his door, at the very hour
Heard bitter doctrine descending on the world.

John Crowe Ransom

Features of Creatures

"Fool, Fool," said Abbott again, and turned that
    name
Outward upon a world of pretty creatures
With rooks' pleasant voices and rats' sweet features,
Born of their mothers noble yet sunk in shame,
Mouthing and nosing, flapping and creeping to
    fame,—
Inward upon himself, if in their faithless ways
He'd sniffed at gold, love, glory in other days
Or anywise had forgot to honor his Dame.

But Fool had the world said too, because he dwelt
Lone in his tower, long after the occasion
Of minatory Authority's invasion;
The King had gone and Paul restored his right
Yet he clung to his cold and poverty and night
And leaned in the rain; the rain came down unfelt.

John Crowe Ransom

Rain

"Rain is a long susurrance; it is no loud
Clamor, yet mutes the terrible bugles; no night,
Yet darkens the insupportable sunlight
And flame-borrowing bush and feather; it is a cloud,
And cool upon your heads, poor wrinkle-browed
Percipiences! Not true Styx, yet a river
Washing the wounded senses of their fever;
Or like a wall let down, or like a blessed shroud.

"Think of the happy dead men lying in ponds
Filled of rainwater—eyeballs rolling wide
In the comfort of the undusty unlit tide—
Ears flowered green and huge beyond the bawling
That shook the air of earth—tumbled, or crawling
On naked legs among the lily-fronds."

John Crowe Ransom

Wrong

The sire of Paul and Abbott had lain long
In his clammy lodgment of no sunlight nor noise,
With handsome revenues left upon his boys,
And over him having been said much sermon and
    song
And from sweet Christian chimes much Ding, Dee,
    Dong,
And having earned his decease he intended now
To keep it. So the insufferable pow-wow
In his sons' house did him most unfilial wrong.

It pricked him wide awake. He was aware
That his two sons, his own hope and the mother's,
Damaged his name and were notorious brothers,
Paul waxing great and thirsting for the power,
Abbott a death's-head gibing from a tower;
His spectral image writhed as in nightmare.

John Crowe Ransom

Weep or Sleep

"Now I remember life; and out of me
Lawfully leaping, the twin seed of my loins,
Brethren, whom no split fatherhood disjoins;
But in the woman's-house how hatefully
They trod upon each other! till now I see
My manhood halved and squandered, two heads, two
    hearts,
Each partial son despising the other's parts;
And so it is, and so it always will be.

"Yet might it be precarious to weep
With eyes slack-fastened and shake these rusty
    joints;
I am a specter, even if at some points
A father, touched too tender by his issue;
So weak and dusty I perceive my tissue,
I must not crack it—I will turn and sleep."

EDWIN ARLINGTON ROBINSON

Edwin Arlington Robinson

REUNION

By some derision of wild circumstance
Not then our pleasure somehow to perceive,
Last night we fell together to achieve
A light eclipse of years. But the pale chance
Of youth resumed was lost. Time gave a glance
At each of us, and there was no reprieve;
And when there was at last a way to leave,
Farewell was a foreseen extravagance.

Tonight the west has yet a failing red,
While silence whispers of all things not here;
And round there where the fire was that is dead,
Dusk-hidden tenants that are chairs appear.
The same old stars will soon be overhead,
But not so friendly and not quite so near.

Edwin Arlington Robinson

KARMA

CHRISTMAS was in the air and all was well
With him, but for a few confusing flaws
In divers of God's images.   Because
A friend of his would neither buy nor sell,
Was he to answer for the axe that fell?
He pondered; and the reason for it was,
Partly, a slowly freezing Santa Claus
Upon the corner, with his beard and bell.

Acknowledging an improvident surprise,
He magnified a fancy that he wished
The friend whom he had wrecked were here again.
Not sure of that, he found a compromise;
And from the fulness of his heart he fished
A dime. for Jesus who had died for men.

Edwin Arlington Robinson

MAYA

THROUGH an ascending emptiness of night,
Leaving the flesh and the complacent mind
Together in their sufficiency behind,
The soul of man went up to a far height;
And where those others would have had no sight
Or sense of else than terror for the blind,
Soul met the Will, and was again consigned
To the supreme illusion which is right.

"And what goes on up there," the Mind inquired,
"That I know not already to be true?"—
"More than enough, but not enough for you,"
Said the descending Soul: "Here in the dark,
Where you are least revealed when most admired,
You may still be the bellows and the spark."

Edwin Arlington Robinson

HAUNTED HOUSE

HERE was a place where none would ever come
For shelter, save as we did from the rain.
We saw no ghost, yet once outside again
Each wondered why the other should be dumb;
For we had fronted nothing worse than gloom
And ruin, and to our vision it was plain
Where thrift, outshivering fear, had let remain
Some chairs that were like skeletons of home.

There were no trackless footsteps on the floor
Above us, and there were no sounds elsewhere.
But there was more than sound; and there was more
Than just an axe that once was in the air
Between us and the chimney, long before
Our time. So townsmen said who found her there.

Edwin Arlington Robinson

THE SHEAVES

WHERE long the shadows of the wind had rolled,
Green wheat was yielding to the change assigned;
And as by some vast magic undivined
The world was turning slowly into gold.
Like nothing that was ever bought or sold
It waited there, the body and the mind;
And with a mighty meaning of a kind
That tells the more the more it is not told.

So in a land where all days are not fair,
Fair days went on till on another day
A thousand golden sheaves were lying there,
Shining and still, but not for long to stay—
As if a thousand girls with golden hair
Might rise from where they slept and go away.

Edwin Arlington Robinson

NEW ENGLAND

HERE where the wind is always north-north-east
And children learn to walk on frozen toes,
Wonder begets an envy of all those
Who boil elsewhere with such a lyric yeast
Of love that you will hear them at a feast
Where demons would appeal for some repose,
Still clamoring where the chalice overflows
And crying wildest who have drunk the least.

Passion is here a soilure of the wits,
We're told, and Love a cross for them to bear;
Joy shivers in the corner where she knits
And Conscience always has the rocking-chair,
Cheerful as when she tortured into fits
The first cat that was ever killed by Care.

CARL SANDBURG

Carl Sandburg

MIST MOON PEOPLE

THE moon is able to command the valley tonight.
The green mist shall go a-roaming, the white river
shall go a-roaming.
Yet the moon shall be commanding, the moon shall
take a high stand on the sky.

When the cats crept up the gullies,
And the goats fed at the rim a-laughing,
When the spiders swept their rooms in the burr oaks,
And the katydids first searched for this year's ac-
cordions,
And the crickets began a-looking for last year's
concertinas,

I was there, I saw that hour, I know God had grand
intentions about it.
If not, why did the moon command the valley, the
green mist and white river go a-roaming, and
the moon by itself take so high a stand on the
sky?
If God and I alone saw it, the show was worth put-
ting on,
Yet I remember others were there, Amos and Pris-
cilla, Axel and Hulda, Hank and Jo, Big Charley
and Little Morningstar,
They were all there; the clock ticks spoke with
castanet clicks.

Carl Sandburg

MAN AND DOG ON AN EARLY WINTER MORNING

THERE was a tall slough grass
Too tough for the farmers to feed the cattle,
And the wind was sifting through, shaking the grass;
Each spear of grass interfered a little with the wind
And the interference sent up a soft hiss,
A mysterious little fiddler's and whistler's hiss;
And it happened all the spears together
Made a soft music in the slough grass
Too tough for the farmers to cut for fodder.
      "This is a proud place to come to
      On a winter morning, early in winter,"
      Said a hungry man, speaking to his dog,
      Speaking to himself and the passing wind,
      "This is a proud place to come to."

Carl Sandburg

MONKEY OF STARS

THERE was a tree of stars sprang up on a vertical
    panel of the south.
And a monkey of stars climbed up and down in this
    tree of stars.
And a monkey picked stars and put them in his
    mouth, up in a tree of stars shining in a south
    sky panel.
I saw this and I saw what it meant and what it
    means was five, six, seven, that's all, five, six,
    seven.
Oh hoh, yah yah, loo loo, the meaning was five, six,
    seven, five, six, seven.

Panels of changing stars, sashes of vapor, silver tails
    of meteor streams, washes and rockets of fire—
It was only a dream, oh hoh, yah yah, loo loo, only a
    dream, five, six, seven, five, six, seven.

BITTER SUMMER THOUGHTS—No. 3

FIRECRACKERS came from China.
Watermelons came from Egypt.
The horses of the sun hoist their heads and nicker
at the fence where the first old evening stars
fish for faces.
And the light of the eyes of a child at a morning
window calling to an early morning snow, this
too is a stranger among strangers.

The splendors of old books may be counted.
The spears of brass lights, shining in the dawn of
the tugboats and warehouses, throw other splen-
dors.
Yet a corn wind is in my ears, a rushing of corn
leaves swept by summer, it is in my ears, the
corn wind.

WALLACE STEVENS

And the sea as turquoise-turbaned Sambo, neat
At tossing saucers—cloudy-conjuring sea?
C'était mon esprit bâtard, l'ignominie.

The sovereign clouds came clustering. The conch
Of loyal conjuration trumped. The wind
Of green blooms turning crisped the motley hue

To clearing opalescence. Then the sea
And heaven rolled as one and from the two
Came fresh transfigurings of freshest blue.

SARA TEASDALE

Sara Teasdale

ON THE SOUTH DOWNS

OVER the downs there were birds flying,
  Far off glittered the sea,
And toward the north the weald of Sussex
  Lay like a kingdom under me.

I was happier than the larks
  That nest on the downs and sing to the sky—
Over the downs the birds flying
  Were not so happy as I.

It was not you, though you were near,
  Though you were good to hear and see;
It was not earth, it was not heaven,
  It was myself that sang in me.

Sara Teasdale

THE FLIGHT

WE are two eagles
Flying together
Under the heavens,
Over the mountains,
Stretched on the wind.
Sunlight heartens us,
Blind snow baffles us,
Clouds wheel after us,
Ravelled and thinned.

We are like eagles;
But when Death harries us,
Human and humbled
When one of us goes,
Let the other follow—
Let the flight be ended,
Let the fire blacken,
Let the book close.

Sara Teasdale

THERE WILL BE STARS

THERE will be stars over the place forever;
   After the house and the street we loved are lost,
Every time the earth circles her orbit
   On the night the autumn equinox is crossed
Two stars we knew, poised on the peak of midnight
   Will reach their zenith; stillness will be deep—
There will be stars over the place forever,
   There will be stars forever, while we sleep.

Sara Teasdale

PICTURES OF AUTUMN

An End

I HAVE no heart for any other joy,
　The drenched September day turns to depart,
And I have said good-bye to what I love,
　With my own will I vanquished my own heart.

On the long wind I hear the winter coming—
　The window-panes are cold and blind with rain;
With my own will I turned the summer from me,
　And summer will not come to me again.

Sara Teasdale

II

Arcturus

WHEN in the gold October dusk I saw you near to
        setting,
    Arcturus, bringer of spring,
Lord of the summer nights, leaving us now in au-
        tumn,
    Having no pity on our withering;

Oh then I knew at last that my own autumn was
        upon me,
    I felt it in my blood,
Restless as dwindling streams that still remember
    The music of their flood.

There in the thickening dark a wind-bent tree above
        me
    Loosed its last leaves in flight—
I saw you sink and vanish, pitiless Arcturus,
    You will not stay to share our lengthening night.

Sara Teasdale

III

Fontainebleau

INTERMINABLE palaces front on the green parterres,
    And ghosts of ladies lovely and immoral
Glide down the gilded stairs;
    The high cold corridors are clicking with the heel-
        taps
That long ago were theirs.

But in the sunshine, in the vague autumn sunshine,
    The geometric gardens are desolately gay;
The crimson and scarlet and rose-red dahlias
    Are painted like the ladies who used to pass this
        way
With a ringleted monarch, a Henry, or a Louis,
    On a lost October day.

The aisles of the garden lead into the forest,
    The aisles lead into autumn, a damp wind grieves;
Ghostly kings are hunting, the boar breaks cover,
    But the sounds of horse and horn are hushed in
        falling leaves,
Four centuries of autumns, four centuries of leaves.

Jean Starr Untermeyer

MIDNIGHT VISION

A silver wind flew by our house
And where it flew I do not know.
But I saw my youth ride by in its hair,
My youth all poised with slender wing
And a crimson heart that burned for life.

A crimson heart that burned for life
Far more than it could yearn for Heaven;
A crimson heart that burned for life
Far more than it could strive for Art.

And yet I know that heart is shrouded
In a milky veil of a dream of Heaven;
And yet I know that heart is locked
In a steely armor forged for Art.

But how do I know I shall surely die
Unless I run with fleetest foot
And bring me back my crimson heart,
My dauntless heart that burned for life
Far more than it could yearn for Art
And more than it could burn for Heaven.

Jean Starr Untermeyer

CATHARSIS

'Tis true she was rejected and cast out
By her own self upon a barren hill,
Where sun-rays seared and where rains beat until
She writhed and panted as beneath a knout.
And when her pain had wrung a final shout
She lay there broken and was very still,
Vised in an agony beyond her skill
To ease or heighten—or to think about.

But with her demons flayed, her sins unhoused,
She was a vessel whose transparence showed
Within its depths a struggling flame that roused
Itself by endless striving, till it glowed
Within her proudest gesture, humblest mood,
And purified the ground on which she stood.

Jean Starr Untermeyer

NATURE CURE

TELL it again in stronger tones
And make your meaning plain:
White cliff, that stabs the water's side
Without the crease of pain.

You gallant maple, teasing birch,
And ruffled, stately pine,
There is a sturdy sap in you—
Share it, let it be mine.

Resistless grass, to every wind
And every scuffling tread,
You yield and bend a patient back.
So let me bow my head.

And you, dear lake, whose candid gaze
Resists my importunate soul,
You hide a secret in your depths—
Deliver it to me whole.

Invite me in and let me work
In that great pattern, planned
In beauty I must kneel before
But cannot understand.

UNDEDICATED

THE very sounding of her name
Contracts my throat like searing flame,
My heart beats heavy and too strong
As hidden tears exalt her song,
Her mind unchained, her racing blood
That lifts a lyric like a flood.
Gold trumpet she, but shoulder-flung,
And put to lip, or thrown to dung
By any lad whose vanity
Hears in her lovely note his cry. . . .
But I'm a steel held scabbard-straight
And tempered long against my fate.
Oh, she may be the Horn of the Lord
But I will be his Sword—his Sword!

LOUIS UNTERMEYER

Louis Untermeyer

DISENCHANTMENT

HERE is the German
  Fairy forest;
And here I turn in,
  I, the poorest
Son of an aging
  Humble widow.
The light is fading;
  Every shadow
Conceals a kobold,
  A gnome's dark eye,
Or even some troubled
  Loreley.
A ruined castle
  Invites me to prowl;
Its only vassal
  A frightened owl
(Most likely a princess
  Under a spell)—
And what light dances
  Behind that well?
Perhaps great riches
  Are hidden there,
Perhaps a witch's
  Magic snare.
I walk up boldly,
  Though my breath falters;
But no one holds me,
  Nothing alters

Except the dying
  Phosphorescence
Where the rocks lie in
  Broken crescents.
These rocks are haunted
  Everyone says,
And here the enchanted
  Dragon obeys
Only the youngest
  Son of a widow
Who waits the longest,
  Fearing no shadow
Of any uncommon
  Phantom in metal,
But dares to summon
  The Thing to battle.
I've said my vespers,
  I've tightened my gloves;
The forest whispers
  And chuckles and moves.
Darker and closer
  The stillness surges—
Not even the ghost of
  A rabbit emerges.
I rattle my weapons,
  I call and I call. . . .
But nothing happens,
  Nothing at all.

  Nothing at all.

Louis Untermeyer

THE DARK CHAMBER

THE brain forgets but the blood will remember.
There, when the play of sense is over,
The last low spark in the darkest chamber
Will hold all there is of love and lover.

The war of words, the life-long quarrel
Of self against self will resolve into nothing;
Less than the chain of berry-red coral
Crying against the dead black of her clothing.

What has the brain that it hopes to last longer?
The blood will take from forgotten violence,
The groping, the break of her voice in anger.
There will be left only color and silence.

These will remain, these will go searching
Your veins for life when the flame of life smoulders:
The night that you two saw the mountains marching
Up against dawn with the stars on their shoulders—

The jetting poplars' arrested fountains
As you drew her under them, easing her pain—
The notes, not the words, of a half-finished sen-
      tence—
The music, the silence. . . . These will remain.

Louis Untermeyer

UNREASONING HEART

HERE in a world whose heaven is powder-white,
Where, cased in glass, the branches bear a weight
Too light for leaves and far too cold for flowers,
Nothing disturbs these alabaster floors.
The black stream does not move; it is a vein
Of onyx cropping out, a metal vine
Twisted and thrown away. There is no sound.
Blankets of snow, curtains of snow-flake sand
Bury the footsteps of the one man here.

Here, where the world has died, away from her,
Here, for the fevered mind too long harassed,
Is wintry silence, cooling space and rest.
Waves of a soundless music rise to lift
The unburied thing that lived and even laughed.
And, as a broken life can be made whole
By looking at the slant of one long hill,
In this eternity of peace, the heart
Forgetting all, forgets that it can hurt. . . .

And yet does even the weariest heart want peace?
Back to the fever, the intemperate pace,
Back to the ruthless word, the headlong deed
(Fearing that passion stilled is passion dead),
The worn heart hungers. . Forever unappeased,
Forever self-persuaded, self-opposed,
It turns away from each escape to pine
212

For the old wars and victories of pain;
Running to all that reason hopes to leave,
With no less hurt and even greater love.
As though to cry, "Here I belong—I must!
Here is the place where I have suffered most."

Louis Untermeyer

ASH WEDNESDAY

(*Mödling*)

I

Shut out the light or let it filter through
These frowning aisles as penitentially
As though it walked in sackcloth. Let it be
Laid at the feet of all that ever grew
Twisted and false, like this rococo shrine
Where cupids smirk from candy clouds and where
The Lord, with polished nails and perfumed hair,
Performs a parody of the divine.

The candles hiss, the organ-pedals storm.
Writhing and dark, the columns leave the earth
To find a lonelier and darker height.
The air grows dingy while the human swarm
Struggles against the impenitent body's mirth.
Ashes to ashes. . . . Go! . . . Shut out the light!

Louis Untermeyer

Clouds of pale cardboard
Creak through the sky;
While, with a hard, bored
Baffled eye,
We turn from these mobile
Toys that are offered,
Seeking a noble
Phrase that has suffered.
But in this airless
Vacuum
Nothing so careless
Can ever come.
Never a burden,
A cry or a curse,
Can hope to be heard in
This crackling verse.
Its one endeavor
Is to be smooth;
Hard and clever,
Its highest truth.
Without a blunder
It stiffens and dies—
What might have been wonder
Is scarcely surprise.

Louis Untermeyer

YET NOTHING LESS

THIS is the top. Here we can only go
Back to the world, that Lilliput below:
A child's toy village scattered in the snow.

What have we come for then? This scornful height
Scarce moved an inch to meet us. Black and white
Seem colder still in this ash-ivory light.

What saves these frozen trees from coming out
And waving threatening arms as though in doubt
Of what it is that we have come about?

What gives these common curves, these hills that
    part
As casually as schoolboys, power to start
Cries from the lips and tears within the heart?

Nothing so much, perhaps, yet nothing less
Than that which wintry earth knows to express:
Love that no longer lives on loveliness.

ELINOR WYLIE

Elinor Wylie

"When you are skimming the wrinkled cream
    And your ring clinks on the pan,
You'll say to yourself in a pensive dream,
    'How wonderful a man!'

"When I am slitting a fish's head
    And my ring clanks on the knife,
I'll say with thanks, as a prayer is said,
    'How beautiful a wife!'

"And I shall fold my decorous paws
    In velvet smooth and deep,
Like a kitten that covers up its claws
    To sleep and sleep and sleep.

"Like a little blue pigeon you shall bow
    Your bright alarming crest;
In the crook of my arm you'll lay your brow
    To rest and rest and rest."

Will he never come back from Barnegat
    With thunder in his eyes,
Treading as soft as a tiger cat,
    To tell me terrible lies?

Elinor Wylie

KING'S RANSOM

About the Emperor's thumb revolving,
Mouthed by Manchu's enamelled dragon;
Upon the damasked barge, dissolving
Within the deep Egyptian flagon;

Downcast before the swine by Circe;
Poised between double diamond prisms;
Clipped by the horseshoe nail that hearsay
Declares a cure for rheumatisms;

If the artificer be Vulcan
Or microscopical Cellini
To set an eyeball for a falcon
Or carve a button for a genie,—

And whether cupped in gold or copper,
In frigid silver or the burly
Embrace of bronze; stained by the upper
Cloud colors, or profound sea-pearly,—

Whether consuming or congealing
In fire or salt, O never shall you
Find an enchantment for concealing
This little moon's enormous value!

Elinor Wylie

A STRANGE STORY

WHEN I died in Berners Street
I remember well
That I had lights at head and feet
And a passing bell.

But when I died in Hounsditch
There came to lay me out
A washerwoman and a witch;
The rats ran about.

When I died in Holborn
In an old house and tall
I know the tapestry was torn
And hanging from the wall.

When I died in Marylebone
I was saying my prayers;
There I died all alone
Up four flights of stairs.

But when I died near Lincoln's Inn
The small gold I had
Surrounded me with kith and kin;
I died stark mad.

When I died in Bloomsbury
In the bend of your arm
At the end I died merry
And comforted and warm.

Elinor Wylie

CONFESSION OF FAITH

I LACK the braver mind
That dares to find
The lover friend, and kind.

I fear him to the bone;
I lie alone
By the beloved one,

And, breathless for suspense,
Erect defense
Against love's violence

Whose silences portend
A bloody end
For lover never friend.

But, in default of faith,
In futile breath,
I dream no ill of Death.

Elinor Wylie

PETER AND JOHN

TWELVE good friends
Walked under the leaves
Binding the ends
Of the barley sheaves.

Peter and John
Lay down to sleep
Pillowed upon
A haymaker's heap.

John and Peter
Lay down to dream.
The air was sweeter
Than honey and cream.

Peter was bred
In the salty cold.
His hair was red
And his eyes were gold.

John had a mouth
Like a wing bent down.
His brow was smooth
And his eyes were brown.

Peter to slumber
Sank like a stone,
Of all their number
The bravest one.

John more slowly
Composed himself,
Young and holy
Among the Twelve.

John as he slept
Cried out in grief,
Turned and wept
On the golden leaf:

"Peter, Peter,
Stretch me your hand
Across the glitter
Of the harvest land!"

"Peter, Peter,
Give me a sign!
This was a bitter
Dream of mine,—

"Bitter as aloes
It parched my tongue.
Upon the gallows
My life was hung.

"Sharp it seemed
As a bloody sword.
Peter, I dreamed
I was Christ the Lord!"

BIBLIOGRAPHY

(The following lists include poetical works only)

CONRAD AIKEN
Earth Triumphant	The Macmillan Company	1914
Turns and Movies	Houghton Mifflin Company	1916
The Jig of Forslin	The Four Seas Company	1916
Nocturne of Remembered Spring	The Four Seas Company	1917
The Charnel Rose	The Four Seas Company	1918
The House of Dust	The Four Seas Company	1920
Punch: the Immortal Liar	Alfred A. Knopf	1921
Priapus and the Pool	Dun..ter House	1922
The Pilgrimage of Festus	Alf. ed A. Knopf	1924

WILLIAM ROSE BENET
Merchants from Cathay	The Century Company	1913
The Falconer of God	Yale University Press	1914
The Great White Wall	Yale University Press	1916
Perpetual Light	Yale University Press	1919
Moons of Grandeur	George H. Doran Company	1921

H. D.
Sea Garden	Houghton Mifflin Company	1916
Hymen	Henry Holt and Company	1921
Heliodora	Houghton Mifflin Company	1924
Collected Poems	Boni and Liveright	1925

T. S. ELIOT
Poems	Alfred A. Knopf	1920
The Waste Land	Boni and Liveright	1922

JOHN GOULD FLETCHER
Fire and Wine	Grant Richards (London)	1913
The Dominant City	Max Goschen (London)	1913
Fool's Gold	Max Goschen (London)	1913
The Book of Nature	Constable & Co. (London)	1913

245

JOHN GOULD FLETCHER (*Continued*)

Visions of the Evening	Erskine Macdonald (London)	1913
Irradiations	Houghton Mifflin Company	1915
Goblins and Pagodas	Houghton Mifflin Company	1916
Japanese Prints	The Four Seas Company	1918
The Tree of Life	The Macmillan Company	1919
Breakers and Granite	The Macmillan Company	1921
Preludes and Symphonies	Houghton Mifflin Company	1922

ALFRED KREYMBORG

Mushrooms	John Marshall Co., Ltd.	1916
Plays for Poem-Mimes	The Other Press	1918
Blood of Things	Nicholas L. Brown	1920
Plays for Merry Andrews	The Sunwise Turn	1920
Less Lonely	Harcourt, Brace and Company	1923

VACHEL LINDSAY

Rhymes to be Traded for Bread	Privately Printed; Springfield, Illinois	1912
General William Booth Enters Into Heaven	Mitchell Kennerley	1913
The Congo and Other Poems	The Macmillan Company	1915
The Chinese Nightingale	The Macmillan Company	1917
The Golden Whales of California	The Macmillan Company	1920
Collected Poems	The Macmillan Company	1923

AMY LOWELL

A Dome of Many-Colored Glass	Houghton Mifflin Company	1912
Sword Blades and Poppy Seed	The Macmillan Company	1914
Men, Women and Ghosts	The Macmillan Company	1916
Can Grande's Castle	The Macmillan Company	1918
Pictures of the Floating World	The Macmillan Company	1919
Legends	Houghton Mifflin Company	1921
A Critical Fable	Houghton Mifflin Company	1922

EDNA ST. VINCENT MILLAY

Renascence	Mitchell Kennerley	1917
A Few Figs from Thistles	Frank Shay	1920

Bibliography

EDNA ST. VINCENT MILLAY (*Continued*)

The Lamp and the Bell	Frank Shay	1921
Aria Da Capo	Mitchell Kennerley	1921
Second April	Mitchell Kennerley	1921
The Harp-Weaver and Other Poems	Harper & Brothers	1923

JOHN CROWE RANSOM

Poems about God	Henry Holt and Company	1919
Grace after Meat	The Hogarth Press (London)	1924
Chills and Fever	Alfred A. Knopf	1924

EDWIN ARLINGTON ROBINSON

The Torrent and The Night Before	Privately Printed, Gardiner, Maine	1896
The Children of the Night	Richard G. Badger	1897
Captain Craig	Houghton Mifflin Company	1902
The Town Down the River	Charles Scribner's Sons	1910
Captain Craig (*Revised Edition*)	The Macmillan Company	1915
The Man Against the Sky	The Macmillan Company	1916
Merlin	The Macmillan Company	1917
Lancelot	Thomas Seltzer	1920
The Three Taverns	The Macmillan Company	1920
Avon's Harvest	The Macmillan Company	1921
Collected Poems	The Macmillan Company	1921
Roman Bartholow	The Macmillan Company	1923
The Man Who Died Twice	The Macmillan Company	1924
Dionysus in Doubt	The Macmillan Company	1925

CARL SANDBURG

Chicago Poems	Henry Holt and Company	1916
Cornhuskers	Henry Holt and Company	1918
Smoke and Steel	Harcourt, Brace and Company	1920
Slabs of the Sunburnt West	Harcourt, Brace and Company	1922

WALLACE STEVENS

Harmonium	Alfred A. Knopf	1923

SARA TEASDALE

Sonnets to Duse	The Poet Lore Company	1907

Bibliography

SARA TEASDALE (*Continued*)
Helen of Troy and Other
  Poems   G. P. Putnam's Sons   1911
Rivers to the Sea   The Macmillan Company   1915
Love Songs   The Macmillan Company   1917
Flame and Shadow   The Macmillan Company   1920
Flame and Shadow (*Re-*
  vised)   Jonathan Cape (London)   1924

JEAN STARR UNTERMEYER
Growing Pains   B. W. Huebsch   1918
Dreams Out of Darkness   B. W. Huebsch   1921

LOUIS UNTERMEYER
The Younger Quire   Moods Publishing Com-
                             pany   1911
First Love   Sherman French & Com-
                             pany   1911
Challenge   The Century Company   1914
"— and Other Poets"   Henry Holt and Company 1916
The Poems of Heinrich
  Heine   Henry Holt and Company 1917
These Times   Henry Holt and Company 1917
Including Horace   Harcourt, Brace and Com-
                             pany   1919
The New Adam   Harcourt, Brace and Com-
                             pany   1920
Heavens   Harcourt, Brace and Com-
                             pany   1922
The Poems of Heinrich
  Heine (*Revised*)   Harcourt, Brace and Com-
                             pany   1923
Roast Leviathan   Harcourt, Brace and Com-
                             pany   1923

ELINOR WYLIE
Nets to Catch the Wind   Harcourt, Brace and Com-
                             pany   1921
Black Armour   George H. Doran Com-
                             pany   1923